Debra Allcock T~

IT'S TOUGH AT THE TOP

The No-fibbing Guide to Leadership

DIRECTORY OF SOCIAL CHANGE

Published by
Directory of Social Change
24 Stephenson Way
London NW1 2DP
Tel. 08450 77 77 07; Fax 020 7391 4804
E-mail publications@dsc.org.uk
www.dsc.org.uk
from whom further copies and a full books catalogue are available.

Directory of Social Change is a Registered Charity no. 800517

First published 2006

ISBN-10 1 903991 69 2
ISBN-13 978 1 903991 69 5

British Library Cataloguing in Publication Data
A catalogue record for this book is available from the British Library

Illustrations by Grizelda
Cover designed by Kate Bass and Simon Parkin
Typeset by Linda Parker
Printed and bound by Page Bros., Norwich

All other Directory of Social Change departments in London:
08450 77 77 07

Directory of Social Change Northern Office:
Federation House, Hope Street, Liverpool L1 9BW
Courses and conferences 08450 77 77 07
Research 0151 708 0136

Contents

Dedication

For the staff and trustees at DSC – for making it less tough
than it could be.

But mostly for Duncan, who makes everything possible.

Acknowledgements

There are many people who have informed and inspired me, not least those chief execs and senior staff who I have spent time with either through networking or training events over the last few years. I am sorry I can't name you all and forgive me if I have missed you out. There are some in particular who I would like to specifically mention.

Jeanette Allen
Deborah Annetts
Neil Betteridge
Lindsay Boswell
Ian Bruce
Rodney Buse
William Butler
Kevin Curley
Susan Daniels
Fiona Dawe
Kathleen Duncan
Fiona Ellis
Quentin Elston
Andrew Forrest
Diana Garnham

Andrew Hind
Simon Kelson
Linda Laurance
Deborah Layde
Ian Lawson
Archie Lightfoot
Margaret Lloyd
John Low
Sheridan Maguire
Linda McGowan
Tony Morgan
Maria Pemberton
Fiona Reynolds
Pat Ryan
Frank Steer

About the author

Debra is the Chief Executive of the Directory of Social Change (DSC). Providing an independent voice for positive social change, DSC is a publishing and training organisation working to help the not-for-profit sector become more effective. Current campaigns include the need to promote transparency and accountability of the sector, the need to increase public confidence in charitable organisations and concern about the sector's independence from government. With a turnover of around £3 million, DSC has contact with some 20,000 voluntary and community organisations every year through its programmes.

Debra also trains, facilitates and coaches boards, chief executives and their top teams in governance issues, leadership, vision, mission, values and the establishment of strategic objectives. She is a trustee of MedicAlert® which is the only non-profit-making, registered charity providing a life-saving identification system for individuals with hidden medical conditions and allergies.

Prior to DSC, Debra was Director and co-founder of 'from small acorns' ltd, a training and consultancy company working on organisational culture change and individual development. During her twenty-one-year career, she has worked in insurance, management consultancy and the voluntary sector, carrying out a range of managerial and leadership roles including sales, product development, media relations and training.

She is an internationally published author of several books covering topics such as leadership, management, communication skills, personal development and time management, and has made many appearances on radio, TV and in the press.

Foreword

As someone who has had 20 years of experience in leadership I am really pleased to be writing this foreword. I have seen the best and the worst of leadership in all three primary sectors – public, private and voluntary. One of the things I have noticed is that whilst there are thousands of standard texts on leadership, there are very few that are both easy to read and offer practical advice that can be implemented in the real world. This is particularly true of leadership texts aimed specifically at voluntary sector organisations.

There is plenty of guidance out there for dealing with the technical side of leadership – but I know that the biggest challenge is the human side of the equation. We need to be clear about the distinction between leadership and management. We know that both are vital components for a senior leader in order to engage people in the purpose of the organisation, but also have the right resources, measures and drills to support and embed their energy and transform it into outcomes.

So many texts deal with the 'ideal' whilst not giving enough attention to what happens in 'real life'. This is why, in my view, a book of this nature is so timely. At a time when more is being asked of leaders in the voluntary sector, when the nature of the 'business' is changing rapidly, when more is being asked, when there is fierce competition for funding and many are losing out, what will give an organisation the edge? Practical, real, focused leadership.

Leadership at the top is hard; it's lonely and highly pressurised. I hope that the good advice offered in this guide will help senior leaders to feel inspired and motivated about their leadership and what they can do to be even better – and of course remain sane!

Ian Lawson
Business Development Director
The Campaign for Leadership at The Work Foundation

Introduction

People have more need for models than for critics.
Scott Simmerman, US management consultant

This book is not big and it's not clever. It is an attempt to look at leadership of a charity or voluntary organisation in the context of the typical problems that are encountered by chief executives and senior staff. We are so used to looking at our world, particularly our working world, *through* the lens of leadership that we can forget to look *at* the lens itself. In a sense this book is about the lens of leadership.

I make no apologies for having 'borrowed' other people's ideas and solutions. This book is not designed to deliver highly original insight into the world of leading at the top. It is deliberately about sharing ideas, thoughts, experiences and solutions of the vast number of thinkers and doers in the world of leadership. It's about those things that I have either seen work in practice or that others have told me work. The content of this book is, therefore, largely drawn from some of the most common issues and experiences in leadership that I have come across, not only in my own personal experience, but also with my work with other chief execs and senior staff in the sector. I have therefore based most of my advice, hints and tips on the ideas and experiences that have been shared with me by hundreds of chief execs and their top teams over the last few years.

I have also deliberately tended to avoid more specific 'technical' information (such as putting together a strategic plan, manipulating your balance sheet etc.) as, in my travels, it has rarely cropped up as a major issue at this level. Most of the stories (both horror and fairy tale), that I have heard, relate to the more human side of leadership – and therefore this is what I have concentrated on.

If you do want more technical information there are a number of texts that are truly excellent, which I list in the bibliography. One of the most helpful and informative is Andrew Hind's *The Governance and Management of Charities.*

As you read this book there will undoubtedly be observations and ideas that you don't agree with or that don't square with your own experience. And there will be things that you don't feel you can implement, for whatever reason. This is perfectly normal and I expect it. In my experience, there is no 'one size fits all' leadership model which can be applied everywhere. Working with voluntary sector organisations and their leaders has shown me that the model required depends on so many different factors – the size of the organisation, its age, its revenue, its cause and so on. Of course, it is highly dependent on the personality, value set and background of you – the person leading the organisation. It is much better to think of leadership as a toolkit, which encompasses all the different models, ideas and approaches. And you, as the leader, take from the toolkit the tool that fits the situation you are currently in. When that situation changes, or if that particular tool didn't work, well, then you try another one.

For some of you, the thoughts, reflections and suggestions will be 'old hat'. But for others they will be new, or at least offer a new way of thinking about it.

I am a big fan of inspirational remarks. Some of the biggest movement in my thinking has been as a result of reading a quote which resonated with me, or hearing an 'ordinary' person say something that seemed truly profound and wise. So I end this introduction with the three quotations that keep me going in the dark reaches of the night! As you read this book, keep these three things in your mind. You might find them helpful too.

This first quote is what makes me keep going when sometimes I feel very unsure about why I am working in the charitable sector at all – or when I wonder if it's really worth the inevitable stress that comes with leading in the voluntary sector.

This is the true joy in life, the being used for a purpose recognized by yourself as a mighty one; the being a force of nature instead of a feverish, selfish little clod of ailments and grievances complaining that the world will not devote itself to making you happy.

I am of the opinion that my life belongs to the whole community, and as long as I live it is my privilege to do for it whatever I can.

I want to be thoroughly used up when I die, for the harder I work the more I live. I rejoice in life for its own sake. Life is no "brief candle" for me. It is a sort of splendid torch which I have got hold of for the moment, and I want to make it burn as brightly as possible before handing it on to future generations.

George Bernard Shaw, 'Man and Superman'

The second quote is the one I read during the times I feel most beleaguered; when my confidence is low, when I am wondering if we are making the right decisions at the right time, or when it really does feel as though I am swimming upstream and the tide against me is the rest of the world! (I know that some of you reading this sometimes have those feelings too – and that I am not alone in this.)

It is not the critic who counts, not the man who points out how the strong man stumbled, or where the doer of deeds could have done better. The credit belongs to the man who is actually in the arena; whose face is marred by the dust and sweat and blood; who strives valiantly; who errs and comes short again and again; who knows the great enthusiasms, the great devotions and spends himself in a worthy cause; who at the best, knows in the end the triumph of high achievement, and who, at worst, if he fails, at least fails while daring greatly; so that his place shall never be with those cold and timid souls who know neither victory or defeat.

Theodore Roosevelt (Paris, Sorbonne, 1910)

The final quote is from an 'ordinary' human being. Ian Lawson, the Chief Executive of the Campaign for Leadership, once said to me years ago, '*The greatest gift you can give to anyone is the gift of an opportunity*'.

This book is my gift of opportunity to you – the opportunity to think, reflect and maybe, just maybe, do something differently.

Read on…

1 What they don't tell you

Upon his royal face there is no note
How dread an army hath enrounded him.
Shakespeare, 'Henry V', Act IV

Outcomes
After reading this chapter you will:
- **Understand the realities of an apparently powerful job title**
- **Have a sense of the behaviours you are likely to encounter**
- **Realise the importance of critical mass.**

The chances are that by the time you read this book you are already at the top or near the top of your organisation. So I'm not going to waste any time asking you whether you are sure you are ready for the challenge! But what I will say is that I believe that leadership is a vocation, not a profession.

Frankly, leadership is a choice. The job title, director or chief executive, does not confer automatic leadership power on you. All it gives you is a certain level of authority, but authority is not leadership. You have to make a conscious choice to engage in the leadership thinking and behaviour that turns a job title into a leadership role.

The job title is a burden more than a blessing

As soon as you gain a job title that implies status and prestige, there will be a number of people, both within and outside your organisation, who will perceive you only through the 'fog' of that job title. They will attribute to you motives that have nothing to do with who you are as a human being, and everything to do with how they perceive senior people.

I attended a 'do' at the House of Commons several years ago. ('Dos' at the House of Commons are common place in the sector! You end up going to an awful lot of them.) I was in conversation with someone when a very senior and well known chief executive of a large national charity came over. He clearly wanted to speak to the person who I was talking to and so simply cut in and completely ignored me. I wasn't offended, particularly, because this frequently happens when you are a woman leader in what is still essentially a man's world (being short and blonde doesn't help either!) and so you tend to ignore it.

Anyhow, my colleague was embarrassed by this and introduced me to this man by name and said that I worked for DSC. He didn't recognise my name (and frankly why should he?). Looking rather irritated at having to speak to me rather than my colleague, he asked me '...are you helping out here today?' He was clearly under the impression that I was part of the administration team. I didn't mind that either, my career began with administrative roles and I think they are massively important and underrated. So, still not being offended, I replied 'No'. To be honest, he didn't give the impression that he really wanted to talk to me so I didn't feel encouraged to open up.

My colleague then told him my job title. 'Debra is the Chief Executive.' You would be amazed at the change in his demeanour then. Suddenly I was someone of importance because I had this job title. Immediately his eyes lit up and his body language changed from dismissive to attentive. That was when I did begin to feel offended. The only thing that had influenced his desire to engage in conversation with me was when he thought of me as somebody important. As an administrator I wasn't worth the time and effort of conversation, as a chief executive I was.

This happens internally too. My current PA, Jill Thornton, is someone who I worked alongside in a different capacity many years ago, and through the vagaries of fate she has ended up being my PA now. So she knows me quite well and has seen me develop and grow over the years. When she took on this current role, one of the first things she observed was that the staff found it almost impossible to see past my job title and that the person they were describing to her was not someone she recognised from her own experience.

So people will have a perception of you that is first and foremost based on your job title. And that perception will be highly influenced by their experiences of senior people in the past and their expectations of how you should or should not behave or act. Good leaders recognise this and take it into account when dealing with others.

Adults not children

One of the things I find both frustrating and amusing when observing leaders in action is how easy it is for them to forget that they employ and work with adults, not children or pupils.

We employ adults who make important decisions in their own lives, decisions that are usually more important in the wider context than those they make at work: where to live; how to educate their children; who to have relationships with; how to manage their money; who to vote for and so on. And yet, these same people walk into work and are asked to sign a chit for a pen out of the stationery cupboard – or are not allowed to make on-the-spot decisions to help out or serve a beneficiary/service user/volunteer or customer because they have to get 'permission'. And so often those permissions are petty, silly things that simply get in the way of the job being done.

Somehow there is a two-way perception that leaders are supposed to be better, wiser and more knowledgeable than the people who they are leading. But how can they be? How can you be? The range of things that you are concerned with as you become more senior in an organisation is so wide that you cannot be expert in any of them anymore. Your job is to employ the experts – and not just to advise you on what decisions you should take – to actually take the decisions about the areas in which they are expert. Your job is to surround yourself with people who know what they are doing and create an environment that helps them to shine. So many leaders behave like either teachers or parents and then get surprised and upset when their staff or volunteers behave like children or rebellious students!

The chief executive I admire the most is a guy called Tony Morgan. He used to say that 'good leadership is about giving other people the space to show up'. In other words, letting them shine.

People not resources

In your organisation everyone is important. On many days they are more important than you. In my own organisation, when we have a lot of people in our building, the most important person is Carole Sandman, our Facilities Assistant, because she has to make sure they are fed and watered. And she is the one who needs to make the decisions on that day about that work. She sees more of our customers than any other person in the entire organisation and she therefore has a bigger influence on how they perceive us and what we do than anyone else, including me.

You need to develop a deep sense of appreciation for the efforts and aspirations of others in your organisation. The best leaders I have come across really, really do believe that they are not better than anyone else and will openly acknowledge that others are more skilled and experienced in particular areas. This is not paying lip service – it is the truth. And if it isn't the truth, if you really are appointing people into jobs that they don't do better than you, then you have to ask yourself *why* you aren't appointing more capable people.

Lots of chief execs say that they can't get the quality of staff they want because of the low levels of pay in the sector. Well, there may be something in that, and if it's true for you, then do something about the pay levels – it's a slow process, but believe me it can be done. Regardless of that, however, the pay isn't so low that you can't attract bright young things at the start of their careers, or older people who want to move out of the corporate or public sector to make a different kind of contribution in their working lives. There are a lot of skilled, intelligent, capable people out there who are not solely driven by the salary. My point is that, quite often, the problem is not one of skill versus no skill, or experience versus no experience, but one of 'I'm the boss and can't let go' versus 'we pay you to be the expert so I *will* let go'. Be honest with yourself – is it you who is preventing them from being fabulous, even inadvertently?

You're not really human any more

The reality is that when you aspire to lead others you will largely cease to be seen as a human being with the same fears, worries, hang-ups and hopes as them. Even though you probably feel all too human and fallible, most people both want and deserve a leader who they can look up to. That doesn't mean that they will always like you. Being moaned about behind your back is actually part of

the job description! But they need someone who they believe deep down, when push comes to shove, can lead the organisation in the right direction.

The biggest test of your leadership ability is not what people do and say when things are going well (anyone can lead success), it's what they do and say when times are tough.

They will expect more of you in terms of how you look, what you say and how you behave. They will notice your mistakes. They will be alert for any signs of hypocrisy. They will be generally unforgiving of the times when you are, or appear to be, hypocritical or unhelpful or obstructive or… (and even if they forgive they sure as anything don't forget!)

Your nerves and stress levels, if seen by others, will have a disproportionate impact on the nerves and stress levels of those around you. The more worried or stressed you are, the more worried and stressed they will be. The more calm and positive you are, the more calm and positive they will be.

They have high expectations, often unreasonable in the context of you as a human being, but completely reasonable in the context of you as the guardian of the organisation, and ergo, their working lives. It means the pressures on you are exceptionally high – and you need to have the strength of character to accept it and deal with it.

Nobody likes you!

So you have to develop a healthy and robust sense of self. You will be criticised, sometimes fairly and sometimes unfairly, the moment you step into a senior role. And this criticism will come at you from all angles. Richard Olivier, in his excellent book, *Inspirational Leadership, Henry V and the Muse of Fire*, quotes from Shakespeare's *Henry V* where Henry is 'walking the job' around the camp anonymously the night before the Battle of Agincourt, listening to the troops talking and complaining about him and his leadership.

After he has listened he talks about how hard leadership is and how often you are blamed for all sorts of things that really aren't your fault.

Upon the King.
'Let us our lives, our souls, our debts, our care full wives,
Our children and our sins, lay on the King'.
We must bear all...
...What infinite heartsease
Must Kings neglect that private men enjoy?

You will find that people around you are judging you constantly. I sometimes think that leadership is a bit like being a politician – people really don't care much about how hurtful their comments or criticisms are – it's free for all in slinging mud! And this judgement will come from trustees, staff, volunteers, partners and of course others in the sector.

An ex-colleague of mine, Steve Prince, shared with me this great saying. 'Isn't it funny how we judge ourselves by our motives and others by their actions?' That pithy little phrase has always struck me as being tremendously useful when thinking about leadership.

You need to develop a thick skin. You need to be able to distinguish between what is justified criticism that you can adapt and use and what is unjustified – where you simply need to acknowledge the criticism and move on. This is not easy and is not really something that you can be taught, it does come with experience. Nonetheless, when hearing the criticism, ask yourself, 'Would I say/ feel the same in that position? Have I ever made similar comments about previous leaders I have worked for or alongside?' Are you over-reacting to someone's tone and manner and is your tone and manner 'upping the ante'?

Critical mass

The larger your organisation, the harder it is to win everyone over to the direction in which you want to take the organisation. Inevitably there will be those who don't agree. Sometimes that disagreement will be healthy and valid. Sometimes it will simply consist of those people who are generally resistant to change. And occasionally it will be those people who, for whatever reason, simply want to oppose anything that you try to do because they don't think that you are right for the organisation.

It is too easy in those circumstances to spend a great deal of time and energy on the, often small, minority who object or complain, and to neglect those people who are energised and optimistic about the future, or who are simply getting on with the job.

As a leader you rarely need unanimity. What you need is critical mass. If the majority of people are with you and what you are trying to achieve then that is usually enough. This means that despite the critics and 'naysayers' (to quote Richard Olivier) the organisation will move forward and this is where you need to be spending your energy. That is not to say that you don't give the others a fair hearing because actually they may have some important and useful points to make – but don't spend a disproportionate amount of energy on those you will never win over anyway.

No one will thank you

Actually this isn't entirely true. But you do need to develop an ability to assess your own performance as a leader and not to rely on others to remind you of what you are good at. Guess what – they won't. You need to know not just what you could do better, but, and probably more importantly, what you do well. An old chief exec of mine, John Garnett, used to say about moving into top leadership positions, 'You can't expect the salary *and* a round of applause!' Fair point. But, can I strongly suggest you find someone who will give you lots and lots of positive reinforcement? I talk more about this is Chapter 9 when I look at how to keep yourself sane.

Patience is a virtue

You will find that things take longer than you either want them to, or think they should. It is one of the endless frustrations of chief execs and, incidentally, trustees too. But the experience of those senior people I have worked with is that things do have a way of happening in their own time. And certainly, you can attempt to accelerate some things. However, unless the ingredients are right, the change process will almost always take longer than you have anticipated.

You will also find that you have to repeat the same messages over and over again, and still people will claim that you didn't tell them! Again, this is a natural function of workplaces, because there are people in them, and they will hear your messages when they are ready to or when you have created the right sort of environment that makes them want to listen. And even then, there will always be those who appear not to have got the message. The ex-Chief Executive of SAS Airways used to talk about 'the thousand tellings'. You have to repeat, repeat, repeat. A simple analogy is when you fall in love and you and your partner tell each other that very first time that you love one another. All well and good – but having it said only once is rarely enough. Even though you know that your partner loves you, you need to hear it often and the same is true of messages in the workplace. Even if people do know something – the vision, progress against objectives, the values, how good they are – they still need to hear it regularly.

So you need to develop the kind of patience that keeps you going when things are not happening as fast as you would like, or when people appear not to have grasped the essentials of your messages.

Failure is inevitable

Many people will judge how successful you are as a leader on how successful the organisation is in that moment, and very often that will be about the money, even though the real test of an organisation in the voluntary sector is about the work that you do. That makes it very easy to concentrate on the now, and to forget what you have achieved and what you are planning to do for the future, because the concentration is on the immediate.

You will of course be criticised if you don't think about the long term, but you will be measured on the now. Despite all that pressure, you need to hang on to your vision and plans for tomorrow, next week, next year and the next decade.

All organisations go through cycles. None simply grow and grow without hitting crisis points. Sometimes it is true to say that the crises come about because of poor leadership, but more often there are external factors that can be hard to anticipate and hard to manage! You need neither to get over-excited or complacent about the good times nor to get over-despondent or worried about the tough times. Both tough times and good times come and go – and come and go, and come and go. 'This too will pass' is a good way of looking at the tough and the easy.

I am reminded of the Kipling poem 'If' and in particular the lines:

If you can meet with Triumph and Disaster
And treat those two imposters just the same…

You can't do it alone

I think, however, that probably the most important thing you need to remember is that you cannot do it alone. You simply must make sure that you have a management/leadership team around you that has established a common set of behaviours and values and that is working with you. It doesn't matter how 'well' you are apparently leading from the top if this is not reflected in what is going on in the rest of the organisation. If the management team is not right, then your best efforts will come to naught. And if the team isn't right, then you simply have to move the members out of the organisation. This is really, really hard to do and I have to admit that I have not done it well myself in the past. I have a tendency to think that I can win everyone over! But trust me, and not just me but your fellow chief execs and senior people – their stories are all similar. If you don't get the right people around you, you will find it extremely difficult to achieve what you are trying to do.

What do I need to succeed?

I believe the single most important quality you need is courage. I penned the following 'Kiplingesque' short poem which I hope illustrates what I mean by this.

The quality which will serve you best
Is courage. So when you are pressed
Around by doubt and fear of what is new,
The courage of conviction will see you through.
Which, in the cold, hard waking hour,
Will hold your hope's inspiring power.
The courage to confess your wrong –
And thus redress, yet show you're strong.
The courage to allow the light
In others, so that they glow bright
Even if this casts you into shade

And no one knows the gift you gave.
The courage to look yourself in the eye
And know your weakness and your lie
And still go on believing in
Your courage to undo your sin.
The courage to speak up for what is right
Even if the ensuing fight
Costs your repute or livelihood,
Still, knowing what you do is good.
And not least of these the courage to know
If it's time to stay, or time to go.

Some critical dos and don'ts!

DO	DON'T
■ Praise	■ Pander
■ Get the right people on board	■ Hang on to people who are not helping you move forward
■ Trust your people and delegate well	■ Try to be the expert yourself
■ Surround yourself with trusted advisers	■ Pay too much attention to the negative small minority
■ Appreciate the people	■ Forget to recognise effort as well as achievement

2 Inspiring or Perspiring?

By working faithfully 8 hours a day, you may eventually get to be a boss and work 12 hours a day. Robert Frost, poet (1874–1963)

> **Outcomes**
> After reading this chapter you will:
> - Be clear about the distinction between management and leadership
> - Have a good sense of your own leadership style
> - Know how to adapt it to help others to follow you.

Are you doing the right things?

In a senior leadership role it is important to distinguish between management and leadership. They are not the same, although they are both equally important.

Someone once said that leadership is about getting extraordinary results out of ordinary people. Someone else said management is about doing things right – leadership is about doing the right thing.

I think these sayings sum up very nicely the difference between management and leadership. Management is essentially about resources, leadership is essentially about people.

The distinction between management and leadership

Managers	Leaders
Set objectives	Create vision
Human resources	People
Motivate	Inspire
Plan	Dream
Analyse	Imagine
Control	Release

The list above shows a polarised version of the difference between the two requirements of senior positions. The popular view at the moment is that leadership is more important than management. I don't share that view. My observation is that you need both. I have worked in my life for two people who had the extremes of management and leadership. One was a superb manager; he followed all the rules and procedures, made sure we had plans, that our work was monitored and so on. The other was an absolutely inspirational leader; we were excited and enthused by his vision and ideas.

Interestingly, under both leaders we, the team, ended up demoralised and actually failing to achieve the task. In the first case, with the excellent manager, we lacked vision and excitement. When things got tough it wasn't enough to know that we were following all the right procedures. We wanted to know why – was it worth it? Sadly, he wasn't able to inspire us in the hard times.

In the second case, the vision wasn't enough. We had no clear plans, no specific objectives, no way of knowing if we were getting there. And, of course, we didn't achieve the vision.

So you need both. A vision is no good without a plan and a plan is no good without a vision.

Why should they follow you?

The American researchers and writers, Kouzes and Posner, talk about leadership as 'a reciprocal relationship between those who choose to lead and those who choose to follow'.

I think this is a useful description for a number of reasons. The first is that it is reciprocal. In other words if people don't follow you then you are not a leader.

Secondly, leadership is a conscious choice. To do the things that make you a good leader requires a commitment and courage greater than that of simply doing what is in the job description.

Thirdly, you can't force people to follow you. They have to choose to.

This is a particular challenge at the top, because you effectively have two tasks to do. You have to create an environment that allows your immediate team (i.e. your direct reports) to want to follow you. But you also have to be credible as a leader to those people further down the organisation who you may not have so much to do with on a daily basis.

Critically, you need to begin with those who report directly to you. If you are providing the right sort of leadership for them, and they are inspired and committed to what you are trying to achieve with the organisation, then they are more likely to disseminate the right sort of positive messages throughout their own teams.

So what makes people want to choose to follow you? When I run my leadership training courses, I ask people to visualise the best leader they have ever worked for, someone who helped to make coming to work a pleasure, who made being committed and enthusiastic easy. Typically the lists look something like this:

Best Leader		
- Listener	- Focused	- Good communicator
- Enthusiastic	- Honest	- Didn't take credit for
- Open	- Didn't get angry	others' ideas
- Sense of humour	about mistakes	- Praised frequently
- Commitment	- Let people get on	- Willing to admit
- Trust in self and staff	with the job	mistakes
- Knowledgeable	- Loyal to the team	- Took on other ideas
- Fair		

Do you recognise any of these attributes when you think about the best leader you have ever worked with?

Then I ask people to visualise the very worst leader they have ever worked for – usually this is much easier for them. They often joke that they are stuck for choice!

Worst Leader		
- Unfair	- Doesn't care about	- Status driven
- Lazy	the staff	- Incompetent
- Inconsistent	- Disloyal – Isn't open	- Has favourites
- Doesn't tell the truth	- Operates a blame	- Doesn't take decisions
- Takes credit for	culture	- Knows it all
others' work	- Doesn't lead by	- Doesn't trust the
- Doesn't listen	example	staff

Again, you probably recognise some of the words on this list too.

Now there are a number of points to make about these descriptions. The first is that, if you notice, most of the words are relationship based. In other words they describe the emotional impact of that leader on the individuals describing them. Secondly, very few of the points in either category are about taking decisions, setting strategic objectives, monitoring results and so on. They are nearly all about relationships, how we felt around this person.

As followers, we judge our leaders almost entirely on their impact on us as individuals – rightly or wrongly.

Interestingly, when I ask the question, 'Did everyone in your organisation agree that this was the best/worst leader?' the answer is usually 'No'. If you think about your own examples, there's a pretty good chance that for those leaders who you thought of as good, there were others in your organisation or team who didn't share your view. The same is probably true for those who you thought were terrible.

So what makes the difference? Why do some people see the same leader as either good or bad? The answer is that it's all about perception.

I was doing some coaching work with a chief exec of a medium-sized voluntary organisation working with children with learning disabilities. This individual (whom I shall call Albert for the present), inherited two senior members of staff. One of these (let's call her Paula) thought that Albert was a great chief executive. The other (let's call him Frank) thought that Albert was terrible. Why? Albert, after all, was one individual, not Jekyll and Hyde.

As we worked it through we realised that the difference was one of perception. Albert's leadership style was forceful and direct. He didn't spend a lot of time agonising about the detail – he listened but made decisions very quickly. Paula had a very similar style and recognised that in him. Frank, on the other hand, was much more thoughtful and detailed in his approach. He found Albert hard to work with because he often felt that his views were not being considered seriously enough. When Paula had a one-to-one with Albert it lasted no more than about half an hour and was very action focused. Frank needed more time. He wanted to talk through the documents/reports he had prepared in some detail.

Once Albert had recognised the dissonance between the needs of his two directors he was able to adapt his style to make Frank feel more appreciated. This in turn helped Frank to find a way to follow him.

This issue of leadership style is an important one. You will often find that those people who think you are great appreciate your style and those who don't, don't!

So it's important that you are aware of how you operate, how others operate and how your own style may impact on others' desire to follow you. Those people who you find 'difficult' may only be difficult because they find it hard to follow you due to dissonance between your preferred style and theirs, not because there is any real, deep distance between what you and they aspire to for the organisation.

Below is a leadership style test that I designed in order to help leaders think about how they lead others. I'm not a big fan of psychometric tests because I suspect they are used too much to label people and don't allow for people's ability to grow and learn. So I invented this one myself. It is simply a tool to get you to think. So, unlike most tests of this type, you can cheat – if you don't like the answer it gives you then change your scores!

The point is that there is no right or wrong answer. The purpose of the test is to get you to think about the relationships you have with those you lead (and indeed those you seek to influence) and to discuss what you can do with your own style to adapt it to the needs of others.

Leadership style test

It is important that you fill in the questionnaire before looking ahead at the scoring instructions otherwise you will find that the scoring system influences how you score yourself.

Instructions

Look at one row at a time. Thinking about yourself in a leadership context, give each word a value from **1–4** with **4** representing the word most like you and **1** representing the word least like you. You must have one of each number only in every row so that each row adds up to 10. In other words every line must contain a 4, a 3, a 2 and a 1.

Example

	Score		Score		Score		Score
Funny	4	**Interesting**	2	**Quiet**	1	**Determined**	3

The test

Score		Score		Score		Score
Trusting	Precise		Enthusiastic		Quick	
Confident	Supportive		Careful		Creative	
Imaginative	Forceful		Responsive		Economical	
Methodical	Demonstrative		Competitive		Helpful	
Determined	Persuasive		Analytical		Receptive	
Adaptable	Practical		Encouraging		Courageous	
Objective	Empathetic		Inspiring		Animated	
Generous	Strong-willed		Mischievous		Factual	
Focused	Relaxed		Challenging		Experimental	
Fun	Action-oriented		Relationship focused		Questioning	

Copy your score from the original sheet on to this one, putting the score against the word. When you have done that add up the scores for each shade and mark them against the boxes below. I use colours because I think they are the most evocative indicators – you'll have to imagine them here.

Score		Score		Score		Score
Trusting	Precise		Enthusiastic		Quick	
Confident	Supportive		Careful		Creative	
Imaginative	Forceful		Responsive		Economical	
Methodical	Demonstrative		Competitive		Helpful	
Determined	Persuasive		Analytical		Receptive	
Adaptable	Practical		Encouraging		Courageous	
Objective	Empathetic		Inspiring		Animated	
Generous	Strong-willed		Mischievous		Factual	
Focused	Relaxed		Challenging		Experimental	
Fun	Action-oriented		Relationship focused		Questioning	

	Score			Score
GREEN			BLUE	
YELLOW			RED	

You will find that you have a slightly different score in each box. So what does this mean? Well, if you look at the words in the 'green' boxes you can probably see that they are linked by people or feelings. The words in the 'blue' boxes are linked by facts or information. The words in the 'yellow' boxes are linked by ideas or creativity and the words in the 'red' boxes are linked by action or results. The higher your score in a particular area the more likely it is that your style is dominated by those words.

For example, if your dominant score is 'red', then you probably come across as quite fast, not interested in detail, want to just get on with it – which is fine, except for those people who want to consider the detail, take more time to come to a decision and so on.

The point is that none of the styles is right or wrong. It's just that someone may not respond well to your leadership, not because either you or they are awful (although you might be!), but because your style and theirs differ.

You can sit on your high horse saying, 'Well, I'm the Boss so we do it my way'. But actually, that doesn't work. If you want people to follow you, you need to adapt your way of being with them to what they need – not what you want to give.

Don't think so much in terms of 'do as you would be done by' because that assumes that everyone wants the same as you. A more effective way of thinking is probably to 'do to others as they would be done to' (or something like that!).

So how people perceive your leadership will be highly dependent upon how they see your style. Some will see it positively and some will see it negatively. None of these perceptions is necessarily true about you, but they do reflect how you are seen, and so they are true for the person experiencing your leadership.

The following is simply a summary of how you might be perceived by people with other styles to you.

	When viewed positively could be seen as	When viewed negatively could be seen as
GREEN **Feelings/ relationships**	■ Caring ■ Supportive ■ Interested in individuals ■ Nurturing ■ Cares about relationships ■ Warm ■ Good listener	■ Over nurturing ■ Misplaced loyalties ■ Puts individuals over the task ■ Not letting people grow or make their own mistakes ■ Hangs on to poor performers ■ Too soft
BLUE **Facts/ information**	■ Practical ■ Pays attention to details ■ Gets the facts right ■ Makes clear logical decisions ■ Authoritative ■ Takes time to think	■ Too much order ■ Over attentive to detail ■ Never gets anything done ■ Always plays by the rules ■ Closed-minded ■ Over-focused on facts
YELLOW **Ideas/ change**	■ Enthusiastic ■ Creative – prepared to experiment ■ Fun to work with ■ Open minded ■ Ready to challenge the status quo ■ Looks for new possibilities	■ Addicted to change ■ Starts things and doesn't finish them ■ Lots of initiatives all at once ■ Doesn't get results ■ Doesn't see things through

RED Action/ results	■ Confident ■ Quick ■ Gets results ■ Dynamic ■ Focused ■ Inspiring	■ Action only ■ Not concerned about individuals ■ Doesn't listen well ■ Bullying ■ Doesn't think things through

The above positive and negative characteristics are of course generalisations. All people are different and will have a mix of characteristics. However, determining how you like to lead and recognising that others may have different perceptions about your style may help you to be a more effective leader.

You may use lots of different styles and approaches when you are leading people, but it's still you, your character and your personality. You are simply adopting the appropriate behaviours for the particular moment.

How to use the styles

With your team

Why not get your team to fill in the questionnaire at your next meeting? Have a discussion about what the differences mean and how you can all be more tolerant and understanding of one another. A word of warning, however. Don't ask people to fill it in about each other. People get very hurt if

they think they are being misunderstood and it may be that the perception they have of themselves is widely different to that of others. Much better to get people to self-evaluate.

For groups

A number of years ago we were introducing a new database system into our organisation. This was a fairly radical change and would require our people to work quite differently from how they had in the past, in order to make the most of the new system. When we briefed the project, we had to be sure that we engaged people's commitment by speaking to their particular need.

So we began by explaining that this was a brand new system which would require new ways of working and thinking (the yellow category), and that it was capable of capturing a great deal of data (the blue category) about our customers which would potentially make our service to them better and make it easier for staff to operate (the green category). And of course all of this would mean we would get better results (the red category). All of this we genuinely believed.

The point is that when you are doing your 'big' leadership briefs and you are seeking buy-in, make sure that you are using all four languages. That way you are much more likely to create an atmosphere where the majority of people will feel more able to follow your plan.

For individuals

You don't have to get people to fill in the leadership style questionnaire in order to adapt your style to theirs. Sometimes it is obvious what style people prefer from the way in which they approach you. But the simplest thing is to recognise when your communication with them is not working well and to experiment with your approach until you find the one that works.

Action-centred leadership

The principle of action-centred leadership was developed by John Adair at Sandhurst during the 1960s. Although leadership models have moved on since then, there are many useful aspects of the action-centred leadership model which stand the test of time and will help you to lead your organisation more effectively. Its beauty lies in its simplicity. It describes quite clearly what you need to do, and when, and it should undoubtedly be a key part of your leadership tool box.

Action-centred leadership says that there are three interdependent areas on which leaders need to focus.

The successful leader recognises that these three activities need to be achieved in balance with one another. Over-focusing on the task at the expense of building the team or developing individuals will result in demotivated individuals and a disconnected team – which of course will ultimately affect the task.

Leaders who put the individuals before the task are not leading from a position of strength. You are not the representative of your people – you are their leader and that means that occasionally the task will have to come first and the needs of the team must be put to the back.

You, as the leader at the top of the organisation, need to ensure that all these three things are in place. So you need to make sure, as far as you are able, that you have the necessary systems, processes and resources for the task to be achieved, the individuals to feel developed and recognised and the teams to work together effectively.

The following framework summarises the key activities.

Key Actions		Task	Team	Individual
Define objectives		Identify tasks and constraints	Hold team meetings; share commitment	Clarify objectives; gain acceptance
Plan	Gather information	Consider options Check resources	Consult Develop suggestions Encourage ideas Assess skills	
	Decide	Priorities Timescales Standards	Structure	Allocate tasks Delegate Set targets
Brief		Clarify objectives Describe plan	Explain decisions Answer questions Check understanding	Listen Enthuse
Monitor/support		Assess progress Maintain standards	Co-ordinate Reconcile conflict	Advise Assist/reassure Counsel Discipline
Evaluate		Summarise Review objectives Replan if necessary	Recognise and gain from success Learn from mistakes	Appraise performance
			Guide, train and give praise	

Taken from *The Manager as Leader*, Industrial Society Press, 1989

I find the framework is most useful when it appears something isn't going quite according to plan. A quick look over it will very often show something that may have been missed. For example, if a particular objective isn't being achieved, is it because it wasn't briefed clearly? Were the jobs appropriately allocated? Did you delegate effectively? And so on.

You can translate this relatively simple model for use at the top of the organisation.

Achieving the task
- Clarify the vision and remind people of it constantly.
- Check progress against mission and objectives.

■ Ensure that the organisation's departments/teams have clear objectives that are measurable and are relevant to the bigger picture (i.e. the vision and mission) and ensure that you monitor regularly by asking your line managers to report on progress.

Building the team(s)

I will talk specifically about building a senior management team in Chapter 5. Here I concentrate on your actions as a leader at the top of the organisation to support team building throughout your organisation.

■ Encourage managers to have regular meetings with their teams.
■ Praise team performances.
■ Assess team's progress against team objectives.
■ Involve teams in developing overall strategy.
■ Encourage managers and staff to build in 'fun' time.

Developing the individuals

■ Walk the job (see Chapter 4)
■ Ensure that the organisation has an effective and easy-to-use appraisal system and that managers are implementing it.
■ Set aside money for training.
■ Introduce an acting in absence system so that when a manager is away a member of their team acts for them, attends meetings on their behalf etc.
■ Speak to as many as your staff as individuals as you can (I have a relatively small organisation with only around 45 full-time staff so I have a one-to-one with every single member of staff once a year so that they have the opportunity to talk to me directly).
■ Be prepared, on occasion, to roll up your sleeves and get stuck in. But don't make it a habit. You should not become a resource that they rely on. You need to be doing your job – not theirs!

Leading by example

As a leader you need to set for your people the example you want them to follow. That means you need to practise what you preach. But first you need to be clear about what sort of example it is that you want to set.

The following questionnaire should help you to think about what might be involved. These are just some generic examples of what could be required in setting a good example. Undoubtedly, there will be ones that are specific to your organisation. Where you score low, you need to take action.

Setting a good example

Self assessment – how well do the following statements describe you?

1   I have communicated to everyone what I think good practice is

Low				Medium					High
1	2	3	4	5	6	7	8	9	10

2   I always adhere to what I think is good practice

Low				Medium					High
1	2	3	4	5	6	7	8	9	10

3   I never cancel appointments or meetings with my staff

Low				Medium					High
1	2	3	4	5	6	7	8	9	10

4   My team have clearly set goals which I monitor monthly

Low				Medium					High
1	2	3	4	5	6	7	8	9	10

5   I take accountability for my own and others mistakes

Low				Medium					High
1	2	3	4	5	6	7	8	9	10

6   I am always calm and positive

Low				Medium					High
1	2	3	4	5	6	7	8	9	10

7   I can control my body language so that my staff don't know when I am feeling stressed/negative or tired

Low				Medium					High
1	2	3	4	5	6	7	8	9	10

8   I have a good work/life balance

Low				Medium					High
1	2	3	4	5	6	7	8	9	10

9   I am very clear about my personal philosophy of leadership

Low				Medium					High
1	2	3	4	5	6	7	8	9	10

10 My staff are very clear about what my leadership philosophy is

Low				Medium					High
1	2	3	4	5	6	7	8	9	10

Modelling

At the end of the day, what you are doing by setting a good example is modelling the behaviour you want others to engage in. I would start by thinking of those people who you consider to be good leaders and copy what they did that impressed you. Then consistently model the behaviour you would like others to exhibit. Some examples might include:

- Turn up to meetings on time.
- Don't work late – leave work at the normal time.
- Walk the job.
- Talk positively about situations including negative ones.
- Listen to people – woes and all – and take account of personal details such as children, holidays, hobbies.
- Demonstrate enthusiasm with your tone, your questions and your body language.

There will be others that are relevant to your work situation.

Behaviour

I can remember sitting in on a senior team meeting where the chief executive was talking about a change to the structure of the outreach team and he asked for feedback on his proposed changes. No one said anything, but the director of outreach programmes looked distinctly upset. It was obvious that he wasn't happy. However, the chief exec ignored it on the basis that the director could have spoken up if he had wanted to. And of course he should have done. And he probably wished he had. But, as my grandmother used to say 'if wishes were horses, beggars would ride'.

You won't be surprised to hear that the proposed changes didn't work well; it was obvious from the body language of the director of outreach programmes that he didn't want them implemented.

The moral of the story is question people in response to their body language. If someone is looking negative, ask them about it. You don't have to be confrontational; simply saying something like 'You look a little unsure about this John' or 'You seem unenthusiastic about this Mary' will often prompt people to speak up. People can obfuscate with words, but rarely with body language. And normally, when it's obvious, they really do genuinely want you to ask them what they think. And if you do ask them, they are much more likely to tell you what they have been thinking. If they then say that they're happy with it – well, they are more likely to make it work, and at the very least you will be able to point out to them that when you asked, they raised no problems.

Distributed leadership

At the top of the organisation what you absolutely must do is grow the leadership skills and abilities of your people. And not just the members of your senior team – but all those who show any aptitude in this area. Succession planning isn't about nobbling some poor soul to take over from you once you finally keel over or get booted out! It's about making sure that the skills and attributes needed are shared and grown in your organisation. That means giving people both training and opportunities, particularly opportunities to lead on projects or stand in for their managers.

Part of your planning for the future has to be about making sure that others know how to lead. And if they know how to lead I promise it will make your job as leader much much easier.

And don't forget to keep *thinking* about leadership. Read books and articles, go on courses, network with others doing the same sort of role. Listen, learn and adapt.

Some critical dos and don'ts!

DO	DON'T
■ Concentrate on how you can adapt your style to others	■ Get stuck in only one way of leading
■ Get your team to think about their own style of leading/interacting	■ Assume others can't change their styles if need be
■ Remember there are three areas you need to deliver on	■ Over-concentrate on one particular aspect of team, task or individual
■ Think about what kind of example you want to set	■ Forget to encourage the rest of your senior team to do the same
■ Question people in response to their body language	■ Ignore obvious non-verbal signs of upset or resistance

3 No vision, no insight

If you want to build a ship, then don't drum up men to gather wood, give orders and divide the work. Rather, teach them to yearn for the far and endless sea. Antoine de Saint-Exupéry

Outcomes

After reading this chapter you will:
- **Know the distinction between vision, mission and strategic objectives**
- **Know how to establish what they are**
- **Know how to involve people in creating them.**

One of the key things that you need to do at the top of the organisation is to ensure that there is a vision and that people know what it is. To be honest, I don't think it much matters whether that vision has been developed by you, your trustees or has always existed. Your job is to make sure that there is one, that it is communicated and understood by your staff and volunteers and above all, that you personally believe in it and are committed to it.

There is a lot of confusion about the difference between vision, mission, aims and objectives. Forgetting about the semantics for the moment, essentially there are three things organisations need in order to be successful:

1. A clear idea of what their world will look like if the organisation achieves its dream (i.e. a vision of the future).
2. A specific long-term target to work towards (i.e. the mission).
3. A number of identified activities that people can work on which will help to achieve the mission and ultimately the vision (i.e. the objectives).

Vision

The most pathetic person in the world is someone who has sight but no vision.

Helen Keller

Do organisations really need visions to survive? And what are they really for? Well, actually lots of organisations have lost sight of their vision (if you'll pardon the pun!) and yet continue to operate perfectly well. But organisations that have lost their vision do have a certain number of symptoms – do you recognise any of these?

- General resistance to change.

- General low morale.
- Tendency to want to give up when things go wrong.
- Focus on internal mechanisms.
- Sense that the organisation exists to serve the staff not the beneficiaries.
- Higher than normal levels of gossip and back-biting.
- Too much bureaucracy.

The typical pattern in the voluntary sector is that an individual spots an injustice, wants to help someone or engage in supporting some cause and has a vision about what they want to do about it. So the origins of most voluntary sector organisations lie in the very clear vision of an individual. As the individual succeeds in doing something about their 'cause', typically they begin attracting funding for it. Then they begin to employ people, and as time goes on movement takes place from, for example, one individual wanting to do something to help blind people, to a large organisation, such as the RNIB, a big national charity, employing thousands of people, using lots of volunteers and attracting large sums of money. And it's often along that route that the vision gets lost and the organisation's focus centres on what it is doing rather than why it is doing it.

Visions unite people. Voltaire said, 'to unite men and women you need to give them cathedrals to build'. In other words, human beings need a sense of a higher purpose, something that helps them to believe that what they are doing is worthwhile. And if they share in that vision, that higher purpose, it unites them and inspires them to put in their best efforts. I think the following apocryphal story describes this beautifully.

> *A man is walking along a building site and he comes across three workers who are laying bricks on top of bricks. The first worker is working quite slowly, without a great deal of enthusiasm and has only managed to lay a few bricks. The man asks the worker 'What are you doing?' and the worker replies, somewhat jadedly, 'Can't you see? I'm laying bricks on top of bricks'.*
> *The man continues along until he comes to the second worker who is working much faster than the first and has laid several rows of bricks. He asks her the same question to which the response this time is, 'I'm building a wall'. The man then comes across the third worker who is working at three times the pace of the other two, has built an entire wall, a corner and a window space and is whistling cheerily at the same time. This time the answer to the question is, 'I'm helping to build a cathedral'.*

According to vision consultant, Ben Thompson-McCausland, a vision is an ambitious dream, which is communicable, achievable, memorable and inspirational. Richard Field, ex Chairman of J&J Dyson, says that a vision is stretching, credible, inspiring and memorable.

What all people engaged in working on vision agree is that it is a 'realisable dream' – a desired future state, something to which an organisation aspires. It is the 'why' of the activity that your organisation exists for. It acts as the touchstone.

It is the thing that helps you to identify what your priorities are when making decisions because the decisions you make should be those that are helping you towards realising your dream. Above all it needs to inspire, be memorable and be something that everyone in the organisation can identify with.

One of the key things that all gurus say about vision is that it isn't measurable. It is not an objective or intention and should never be designed or amended by accountants! And it should be expressed in the language of the everyday. People aren't generally inspired by statements such as 'our vision is to ensure a socially coherent, economically vibrant community which minimises social exclusion and maximises effective regeneration of blah de blah de blah...'

For starters, what on earth does that mean? Actually it means a happy, well-off bunch of people who get on well and care about their community, doesn't it? Simple language that touches the heart is the most effective language of vision. Martin Luther King said 'I have a dream...' He didn't say 'I have a re-engineered strategic plan for changing a paradigm'.

For Jews, Christians and followers of Islam, one of the memorable visions was Moses' vision to the 12 tribes of Israel – a land of milk and honey. I've never heard it said that the elders came back to Moses and said 'OK, but only if the milk is semi-skimmed and the honey comes from organic bees!'

A vision is not a business plan. It is a simple statement of what the world will look like once you have finished your work.

A vision is the desired unmeasurable, unquantifiable, future state that you wish your organisation to achieve. Having identified the vision all the other management speak is simply a way of defining how you go about working towards achieving your vision. So you identify a mission (also an aim) which you then break down into specific objectives which are then further broken down into plans.

To return to our Moses example, his vision coming out of Egypt was '...a land of milk and honey'. The mission was to reach the Promised Land and the objectives were things such as getting across the Red Sea and so on.

The vision shouldn't be a strapline. In fact, really the vision is not for people outside of your organisation. It is for your staff and volunteers, in order to inspire them in their daily activities. So you are not necessarily trying to come up with some statement that will please a funder, or a supporter. For these groups of people you express the vision and activity of your organisation in whatever language is going to get you the money or the support. The real vision statement is for you and your people: your staff, your volunteers, your trustees.

I have observed that the most successful organisations are those that have visions that broadly fit the following criteria:

- They are inspiring.
- They are believable – they fit the context of the organisation.
- They feel achievable – even if not in this lifetime.
- They are rarely more than seven to ten words long.
- They are memorable.
- They use simple, everyday language which people can understand and identify with.
- They describe a picture of the future – avoiding 'doing' words.
- They stand the test of time – they are usually big enough to cope with the changing environment in which the organisation is operating.

So, a vision sets the overall context by which individuals can connect with the organisation and help them to create new possibilities. Above all, having a simple vision statement helps you to 'speak possibility into being'. In other words, things become possible that wouldn't have been before because people now have something to work towards.

Below are some examples of visions that I have collected on my travels around the UK voluntary sector. They were developed by the people who worked in the organisations concerned as part of a training programme – so they may not be the official vision of the charity concerned – but they are the visions that inspired the people who came up with them.

Scottish Pre School Play Association
Confident happy children

International Voluntary Service
A world at peace

National Museum of Scotland
Inspired, educated people with a sense of the past

Kibble Education and Care Centre
A future for young people with a past

Scotland's First National Park
Local folk working together in their community

BGWS Fostering Service
A safe place and new future for vulnerable children

Knowsley Community Empowerment Network
Government decisions shaped by the community

Lincoln Welcome Asylum Seeker Support Group
Safely at home in a welcoming city

Soundlincs – Lincolnshire Music Development Agency
Sound opportunities for all

Creative and Supportive Trust
Women ex-offenders leading positive lives

Artangel
People appreciating contemporary art

Cruse Bereavement Care
Life after death

Ely Museum
People with a sense of history

Action for Young Carers
Young carers with a life of their own

Nottingham Central Women's Aid
Strong, confident women

And my two particular favourites!!

Young Single Homeless Project
Yooves wiv rooves (sic)

Age Concern Swansea
Sex and sangria for senior citizens in Swansea

How to create a vision

As you can see from above, the simpler the language and the shorter the sentence the more powerful and inspiring the statement can be for people. So what prevents us from having short, inspiring statements? Usually, trying to create a vision with the involvement of a committee. It is generally best to avoid having too many people involved with coming up with the final wording. This is because people are terribly attached to their particular words and find it difficult to let go. And that's when you end up with a vision statement which is several paragraphs of big, long words that people don't actually understand – but no one wants to say so.

Having said that, however, you do need to *involve* people in the development of the vision. There are a number of reasons for this. Firstly, they will have thoughts and ideas that you don't have, that are likely to make the vision more powerful. Secondly, if they have had no involvement it is much harder for them to buy in to it.

Nonetheless, the final putting together of the words probably needs to be done by you. And at the very least the vision has to be something to which you personally are deeply committed. It shows if you're not.

My advice with developing a vision is to keep the process very simple. The following process works whatever the size of your organisation; you just need to adapt it accordingly.

Stage 1 – Buy in to the concept of vision

Begin with your trustees. Have a conversation with your chair about the vision of the organisation and how important it is that it is still relevant and meaningful. Put an item on the agenda of the next board meeting asking questions along the lines of 'What is our vision currently? Do we all agree with it? Do we all understand the same thing when we hear it? Is it still relevant today?' Ensure that you share with them what the whole concept of vision is about in the first place. Many people confuse vision with mission statements and business plans. Clear that up first.

Stage 2 – Consult, round 1

If you are a small organisation, gather all your people together in one room. If you are larger, get your managers to meet with their teams. Tell them that you are looking at the vision of the organisation, want their help and input and ask questions such as:

- What is special about this organisation?
- What do we want to achieve?
- Who are we trying to serve?
- How do we want the world/their lives to be different as a result of the work that we do?

Gather up the critical words and use them to inform your thinking. Tell people that you will be working on it and will come back to them with further thoughts.

Stage 3 – Come up with a statement

You and maybe one or two others thrash out the statement. With one organisation I worked alongside, the chief exec and the chair of trustees went away and came up with a statement on which they consulted the rest of the trustees. They asked their fellow trustees to focus on the 'spirit' of the statement, that is, what it was conveying, and not to get too distracted by the actual words. This worked well.

Also, don't let the size of the vision scare people into not having one. So many great ideas get scuppered because some bright spark says 'But, if we grow our membership base by 100,000 we won't have the resources to deal with it!' Well firstly, wouldn't it be great if we were faced with that problem, rather than the one of not having enough members! And secondly, if it does grow, you'll also grow the resources to meet the demand. Honestly. You will.

The elders didn't say to Moses (well, as far as I know – I wasn't there) 'What if we haven't got enough cups for people to drink the milk out of? We don't have anything to clean sticky fingers with when they've eaten all the honey!'

Stage 4 – Consult, round 2

Share what you have come up with with your staff and volunteers and ask for their opinions or ways in which it might be amended. Again, focus on the 'spirit' of the statement, not the actual words.

Stage 5 – Communicate infinity times!

Once you have decided what your vision is you need to communicate it over and over again. It needs to be on posters, at the top of internal documents, referred to at staff meetings, team meetings, senior management meetings and trustee meetings. Discuss your ongoing achievements using the vision as the 'backdrop'. Remind people. Remind people. Remind people.

Mission

You will probably either remember, or have heard of, the famous phrase attributed to John F Kennedy, President of the United States during the 1960s: 'A man on the moon by the end of the decade'. Actually, this isn't a vision at all – although it's often quoted as being one. It is in fact a mission or aim. The vision was one that the Americans shared with the Russians, perhaps even the whole of mankind, which was unspoken but nonetheless shared, something along the lines of 'Mankind in space'.

The mission is effectively the single big goal that will help you to achieve your vision. It's like a milestone on the way. So 'a man on the moon by the end of the decade' is one of the things that could be done to help achieve the overall vision of 'Mankind in space'. For the Russians, you could say that the mission was 'a man orbiting the earth' (i.e. Yuri Gagarin).

Missions are always measurable, but again expressed in simple, easy-to-understand language.

For example:
Vision: All children in Barkham have access to a good education.
Mission: To provide all children with learning disabilities in the Barkham area with access to specialised educational help by the end of 2010.

Again, the trick with deciding on what the core mission is is to keep it simple. What's the one big thing that the organisation could achieve which would be a big step towards achieving the vision?

Unlike vision, mission statements are usually measurable and quantifiable. They will frequently have a timescale attached to them.

Objectives

This is much more straightforward as most of us are used to setting specific objectives. Be sure that the objectives are closely linked to the actions that you need to take in order to achieve the mission. If it isn't going to help achieve the mission then you need to test its validity in the context of your own organisation.

For example:

Vision: All children in Barkham have access to a good education.

Mission: To provide all children with learning disabilities in the Barkham area with access to specialised educational help by the end of 2010.

Objectives:

1 By the end of the year to have developed a relationship with the local authority so that they are factoring our proposals into their plans.

2 To create a parents' group for the Barkham area which is attended by at least 60% of those parents whose children could be part of the programme.

3 To develop a range of training materials which help teachers to facilitate the learning of children with special needs.

And so on…

The trick with all this is simplicity. The temptation is to make your plans, including the vision, mission and objectives, look sophisticated and complex, not least because often trustees like that. But at the end of the day your people need to understand what the organisation is trying to do, how it plans to do it and where they fit in.

At DSC, every one of our strategic objectives was taken by each manager, who worked with their teams to come up with the specific things that each department needed to do to contribute to the overall picture. This was then put into a spreadsheet and once a quarter the managers go back to the spreadsheet and update progress. It's a great way of keeping track and a good discipline as it reminds managers, in the midst of the day-to-day hustle and bustle, that there is a larger context in which we are working and that they, and their teams, are a critical part of it.

Summary of key points

Vision	Mankind in space
Mission	A man on the moon by the end of the decade
Objectives	Build a rocket
	Train astronauts
	Invent rocket fuel etc.

Some critical dos and don'ts!

DO

- Involve people in thinking about what the vision is
- Clarify for your trustees and staff the difference between vision, mission and objectives
- Keep the vision simple and inspiring
- Make sure that the mission and objectives are a way of achieving the vision
- Remind people, remind people, remind people

DON'T

- Write the vision by committee
- Get hung up on semantics – so long as you have these three things it doesn't matter that much what you call them
- Forget to keep revisiting it
- Forget to monitor how you are doing against the vision, not just the business plan!
- Believe that putting the vision on a poster or the front page of the strategic plan is how it is communicated

4 Gossip, grapevines and team talks

The greatest problem in communication is the illusion that it has been accomplished.
George Bernard Shaw

Outcomes

After reading this chapter you will:
- **Know how to manage the hidden communication channels**
- **Have some ideas about how to implement formal communication mechanisms**
- **Have a sense of how effective your own listening is.**

Informal communication mechanisms

As someone at the top of the organisation, you are communicating all the time whether you realise it or not. You are constantly being observed. Your behaviour, what you say and how you say it and your general demeanour are being observed and noted, whether consciously or not. This chapter looks at the ways in which you communicate messages, formally and informally.

Organisations are not machines. They are unpredictable in how they behave. And the behaviour of organisations is influenced by the people within them. Self-evident you might say. But what influences the behaviour of the people? The information they gather and the communication processes they use. This is not straightforward. So much communication goes terribly wrong in organisations because we have not thought about what it is that we need to communicate, who needs to know and why they need to know it. Neither have we remembered that in the absence of information from the top, people will 'work it out', and often get it wrong.

I find it useful to think about organisational communication as if it's an ecosystem. Every part of it is connected to every other part in some way, and the whole and the parts are connected to the external world. And often the connections are not obvious or apparent. How is it that something you thought was confidential is being talked about in the corridor? Or something that you thought was fairly straightforward suddenly blows up and becomes a hot topic or source of contention?

Despite all our efforts to 'intelligently design' our communication mechanisms by putting in structures and reporting lines, at the end of the day the structure is only as good as what the people working within it know and understand. That is not to say that it isn't worth spending time thinking about organisational structures, because of course a structure can either support your work or collapse under the weight of it. But the critical thing is to be constantly alive to the hidden structures in your organisation.

What are the hidden structures?

The hidden structures are the informal networks of information that pass minute by minute between people, teams and virtual communities. Most of the culture, environment, work ethic, information, celebrations, heartaches and information that people gather and share is through these hidden structures. Unfortunately, because they feel so nebulous it is too easy to ignore them and focus on what appears to be 'proper' communication channels, such as e-mails and intranet.

Gossip

The first mechanism that supports this hidden structure is gossip or 'the grapevine'. And it is called the grapevine for good reason – because it grows extremely fast, gets into all sorts of nooks and crannies and is very strong! So what is gossip? Well, it's the informal chats that people have by the kettle, in the pub, in the corridor or via e-mail.

People want to be able to talk about each other and particularly about what is happening to them, and of course about their bosses. Part of this talking is to check out what other people think, see if it coincides with their own thinking and jointly to establish what the accepted view of a particular person or a particular situation in the organisation. We all do this.

Human beings are programmed to interact socially. With the exception of the few sociopaths in the world, all of us, even those of us who are Internet and web chat addicts, end up needing human contact. And we are programmed to interact through the medium of gossip. I mean gossip not necessarily in its negative sense (i.e. whispers and hurtful innuendo) but simply people talking about other people.

So we have established that gossip in and of itself is not necessarily deliberately malicious, but a way of building relationships through the exchange of information. Unfortunately, because many of us in leadership roles are oblivious to, or deliberately ignore, its existence, gossip can often get out of hand. And your best efforts to communicate the truth to people can be hijacked by a well-placed piece of gossip.

Gossip tends to get out of hand if there is a lack of information about what is going on from the leadership team of an organisation. That's both formal, set communication as well as informal routes.

You need to know what people are talking about. What is on the grapevine? What is in people's heads? That's not to say you should have spies about the place, although it does help to have someone reliable who will let you know what the general mood is. But in a sense, you actually need to be part of it. I don't mean that you join in the gossip – but you need to be sufficiently well connected to hear what's going on. That means don't lock yourself in the office: hang out in the kitchen with the staff occasionally, go to the pub once in while.

Walk around the building saying 'hi' to people informally. Ask them what they think about a particular issue. Don't restrict all your communication with your people to formal occasions and *do not rely on e-mail!*

Who is your 'political journalist'?

I have recently finished reading the journalist and TV presenter Andrew Marr's excellent book, *My Trade.* Amongst many other useful and interesting revelations about the world of the media, he talks about the difficult balance that political journalists have in trying to 'get close' to politicians in order to really know what's going on whilst at the same time remaining sufficiently independent in order to be objective in their reporting.

He makes the point that if journalists get too close to politicians, they start to gain some insight into what some of the problems are that they face and this inevitably leads to sympathy and understanding, which could therefore blunt the journalist's ability to go on the attack when necessary.

> *...a Chequers invitation...can make the recipient just a little bit more understanding of the problems facing the Prime Minister than he or she otherwise might be... If you really talk with a politician about their in-tray, and the problems of rival departments or dodgy initiatives, it is hard to avoid seeing things their way. The same perspective that gives you insight also blunts your hostility.*[1]

I think this is a useful analogy in organisations generally. You too will have your political journalists: the ones who take what you say and interpret it for the 'masses'. And the less they understand of the real issues that are facing you in leading the organisation, the more likely it is that their interpretations of what you are doing will be negative. You need to make sure that you are explaining openly and honestly what is going on, what you are trying to achieve and why. Make a particular point of sharing information with your 'political journalist'. This isn't about being manipulative, it's about common sense. If you don't tell people what's going on and what the problems are, how on earth do you expect them to be enthusiastic and supportive?

You can identify your political journalists fairly easily. They're often very popular with staff, the ones who are the centre of attention in the pub, the ones who people go to most often to question.

Behaviour

> *The most important thing in communication is to hear what isn't being said.*
>
> *Peter F Drucker, management guru*

The second key mechanism that supports the hidden structures is behaviour, that is, the observed body language, tone of voice and facial responses to information which people notice and which influences how they think about and react to what is going on around them.

The look on your face, the posture of your body, the speed with which you walk through the office, the tone of your voice, all of these things influence what people think. If you look cross and worried then they will assume that there is something to be cross and worried about – and that it's probably serious. If you look positive and enthusiastic, then guess what! They'll assume that there is much to be hopeful about. Do not underestimate the power that your behaviour, expressed largely through your body language, has on those around you.

Not only that, but people believe what they see rather than what they hear. If I was to say to you that this paper is pink with green spots would you believe what I say or what you see? If you want people to behave in a certain way then you need to behave in that same way. There is an apocryphal story about a woman who wanted her son to stop eating sugar. So she took the boy to see Gandhi and asked him to ask her son to stop eating sugar. Gandhi said he couldn't do it then, but asked her to bring her son back in a couple of weeks. When she returned, he told the boy to stop eating sugar. The woman was puzzled and asked him why he couldn't have said that two weeks ago. Gandhi replied that two weeks ago he, Gandhi, had been eating sugar.

Wherever this story came from, it's a great one. If you want your staff to be positive then you have to be positive. If you want them to go home on time then you have to go home on time. If you want them to listen to critical feedback then you have to listen to critical feedback. You will influence more by your general behaviour than you ever will through laying down rules or giving briefings.

Sometimes, you simply need to know when *not* to be seen because in that moment it is too hard to manage your behaviour appropriately.

Don't forget that it's also about your more general appearance. There's no point bleating about how unfair and wrong it is for people to judge others by what they wear. The fact is that we do. Don't distract from your credibility by assuming that you, at the top, can get away with not 'looking the part'. You will switch off more people by not wearing smartish stuff than you will please those who want you to make a statement by wearing scruffy jeans (which in themselves are inviting judgement).

All of this is also true of your senior staff and managers. Do you spend time with them talking about how they behave? Have you discussed how 'information' is communicated simply through what their facial expression is when they walk out of a management meeting? Have you talked about looking the part? When you discuss the messages you are giving your staff and volunteers, do not ignore the hidden messages given out by behaviour and body language because people will believe those messages more than what you say.

We keep hearing Gordon Brown and Tony Blair say that there is no problem in their relationship. But we know there is. How? Because it is screamingly obvious when you observe their body language when they are around each other or talking about each other.

Of all the various things that can help or hinder you in achieving your organisation's vision – these two things, gossip and behaviour, are the ones that, above all else, can absolutely cripple you if you are unaware of them and how they work in your particular case.

Power

There is a third influencer on how things are perceived which I will now discuss. This is about 'power' – who has it, or is who perceived to have it.

It is important that you understand both where the power actually lies in your own organisation and where people perceive it to lie. This is also true of the external environment in which you are operating.

There is a three-dimensional view of power:[2]
1 The power to force someone to do something.
2 The power to influence what someone does.
3 The power to shape what someone wants to do in the first place.

The first is the most obvious power of leadership. Leaders can insist that individuals carry out certain tasks. This is generally the power of authority.

The second is the less obvious form. Certainly the person/people at the top of an organisation can influence how people behave – but actually a lot of that influence will come from their immediate managers or their peer group. This is also the power that is used most effectively in lobbying for change in the external environment.

The third form of power rarely comes directly from the top. It is more often immediately influenced by peer groups, who, after all, are those people with whom we have the strongest relationships and who are the ones we are more likely to trust.

I have taken this principle slightly further and identified some types of power that I believe reside in organisations and have an impact on how effective the organisation can be.

Personal power – This is the power of personality. Some might call this charisma. It is the power of the individual who has, or appears to have, a lot of self-confidence.

Status power – This is essentially the power of position, where the individual is perceived to have high status within the organisation's hierarchical structure.

Resource power – This is the power over money and the equipment, who has it and who can make decisions about where it goes.

Influencer power – This is the power to influence how people think about a particular circumstance, person or set of people – often your political journalist.

Expert power – This is the power of the person who is seen as having all the knowledge or information about a particular subject.

Popular power – This is the power of the person who is well liked by others in the organisation and whose view will be listened to because individuals wish to be liked by this individual or be part of his or her 'gang'.

All the above sorts of power lie with different individuals in the organisation and it is important you recognise who they are so that you can ensure that you are influencing these power sources yourself.

This may sound a little Machiavellian; however, actually it is simply common sense.

Formal communication processes

We have already talked about the need for the chief executive and senior staff to be visible informally. It is also important to be visible formally. This means that you should regularly speak directly with staff in a formal fashion.

In small organisations (say less than 100 people) this is relatively easy to do.

In larger organisations – especially those that are regionally spread, it's a little harder and you need to be slightly more creative in how you make sure you are seen by your people. However, you could do things like attend a different region's meeting each month and give a piece of information about what is going on.

It is important to have some formal mechanisms because people only tend to 'make up' information if they are not given the correct information in the first place.

Internal communication systems and structures

You need to ensure that your people (staff and volunteers) understand what is going on both inside and outside the organisation and that they know if there is any action they are required to take.

There are a number of communication mechanisms that are available to your organisation. Some are more appropriate than others and some work best depending upon the current circumstances.

Still going on the basis that 'she or he who communicates leads' it is important to ensure that you build up communication structures within your organisation that both deliver and gather information and that also reinforce the leadership status of your line managers and team leaders or supervisors. This is why the bulk of communication with staff, in my view, should be done by the line manager of the team/person concerned.

I am going to focus on delivery of information for the moment – because even though you want to engage in a two-way dialogue with staff, there are many occasions when what you need to do is simply impart information.

Of course, your communication structure does depend to a large extent on the size of your organisation and the size of your management/leadership team. Nonetheless there are some basic rules which should stand fast regardless of how large or small your organisation is.

Rules of effective communication structures

- Staff need to know what information they can expect to receive and at what time/date, and that it is a regular repeating occurrence.
- Managers need to know what information is to be communicated and what is not – in particular what the key messages are that need to be put across.
- Staff need to be given information in a context that is relevant to them.

Whilst it is important that you, as someone at the top of the organisation, are seen to be communicating publicly with staff, if the main purpose of your communication is to keep people informed so that they can adjust their behaviours if necessary or take action, then the most appropriate forum for them to do that is usually within their own teams.

In my experience the following basic structure seems to work best in terms of ensuring that the right information is disseminated at the right time. This is based on a concept called 'team briefing' which is a cascade mechanism.

Team briefing – the provision of information

STAGE 1

Senior team meeting
- Once a month agree what are the messages that need to be communicated to staff
- Agree both the 'facts' that need to be communicated and the management 'line' associated with those facts
- A useful structure is around the 4 Ps
  - Progress – how well is the organisation/department doing, what has it achieved etc.?
  - Policy – what new policies/procedures/systems etc. do people need to know about?
  - People – what information is there about, for instance, new members of staff, clients, service users, beneficiaries etc.?
  - Points for action – as a result of the first 3 Ps what are staff/volunteers required to do?

STAGE 2

Managers prepare
- Translate the information gathered at the senior team meeting into something that is relevant to their team

- Anticipate and think about likely questions to ensure managers can answer them or know how to handle them if not
- Managers must publicly support management decisions. If a manager feels unconfident about briefing a particular point or has such strong reservations that they are uncomfortable about supporting it publicly, then this is their opportunity to seek guidance and support from their own line manager

STAGE 3
Managers brief

- Managers meet with their teams and brief the 4 Ps, making it directly relevant to their team wherever possible
- Brief core information as well as information that is 'local', i.e. relevant to that team only
- Build in time for questions, comments and feedback

STAGE 4
Feedback

- Managers communicate back up the line, either immediately or at the next senior team meeting, what the feedback/reaction has been, any questions that have been asked and so on

Note that in stage 1 you are not just agreeing the 'facts' that need to be communicated, but also the management 'line'. In other words – how is the message to be communicated and what behaviours do managers need to engage in during the communication in order to support the line. It is *critical* that you clarify with your managers that they must brief all decisions as if they were their own. In other words, even if they disagreed in the meeting with a course of action, outside of the meeting they have to act and behave positively about that course of action. Be clear that it is not acceptable for managers to say things like 'well, I don't agree with it either' or 'don't blame me, it wasn't my decision'. Make it clear that managers have absolute freedom to challenge and argue during the meeting or with you privately. But once the decision has been taken they must support it, otherwise it undermines not just that particular decision, but the whole of the leadership team.

If, having worked with them on the rationale for the decision/action, they still can't take the management line then you will need to have a long and hard conversation with them about their future as a manager in the organisation. You simply cannot afford to have your managers undermining your decisions and actions. It is completely unfair on staff and volunteers. This can be hard to do, but don't shirk it. If they really can't adopt the line, then they have to go. This is why it is so important to ensure that you incorporate into the job description of your management team clear information about what it means to be a leader/manager in the organisation and what is expected of them.

In stage 2, work with the managers initially to help them to make the information relevant to their teams. For instance, if the main item on progress is that £50,000 has been donated towards a particular project, then the finance manager might talk about the impact on the bank balance, the project manager might discuss the impact on staff workloads and so on.

You will need to ensure that your managers are sharing information appropriately and in the right way, so I strongly advocate some formal training. It is not always immediately obvious to people what is the best way of sharing information, and by being properly trained they are more likely to make a good job of it. This is critical in the context of the performance of the organisation. If people don't know what they need to know, they can't do what they need to do.

With the process I describe above I suggest that there are a couple of days between your senior management team meeting and the managers' briefing with their staff. This gives them plenty of time to prepare.

I also strongly suggest that you ask managers to brief their staff at the same time each month (so that staff know exactly when the meeting is and can organise their work to make sure there are no distractions) and at the same time as each other (so that new information is not passed between teams before they have heard from their own manager, otherwise it can get distorted).

Establish a staff forum

A staff forum is a way for staff to 'gossip' in a more structured way, having an agenda for the discussion which should enable those who disagree with the expressed view to speak up in a relatively safe environment. They will perceive the environment as safe because there are no managers there and they will be less likely to feel nervous about expressing their real opinion.

In my experience staff forums, particularly if they are run well and the right tone has been set at the beginning, are enormously beneficial to an organisation. To begin with, it is unwise to rely solely on feedback from your managers about how staff are in general or how they are receiving/reacting to information/changes and so on. This is not because your managers deliberately tell fibs. It is just that they will hear and report back on the things that matter to them, which may not be the same as the things that you believe to be important, or indeed, that the staff believe to be important. Secondly, human nature is such that we do find it very difficult to be entirely honest with our bosses. There are usually perfectly valid reasons for this: we want to look good; we want to impress our boss; we like them and can see they are under pressure so don't want to add to it; we believe we can handle the problem/situation ourselves and so on. Therefore, your managers' staff are likely to not be entirely honest with them, and your direct reports are, in turn, unlikely to be completely honest with you.

With a staff forum you get feedback directly from staff, without it being interpreted or managed by your middle/senior managers. Staff tend to feel more directly involved in the wider context of the organisation.

When I asked the leader of our staff forum at DSC, Sarah Westlake, what she felt the benefits were of our own staff forum she came up with the following (her words are reproduced exactly).

- 'encourages a free and easy flow of communication between staff;
- encourages debate about processes on a shop floor level;
- when the information gathered is used successfully and acted upon by senior management team it helps the staff feel listened to and that their opinions have worth and gravity;
- really gets ideas moving on how to improve and work with each other, so is innovative;
- helps staff realise what kind of pressures each team is under and can liaise to offer help on the ground;
- when senior management team sets aside time and covers the phones etc. to enable this to happen, it makes staff feel valued.'

We are particularly lucky with Sarah being our forum leader, because, in my opinion, she is highly intelligent and 'grown up' in the way in which she both leads the Forum and handles the sometimes difficult feedback she needs to give to the management team or to me. If you're not lucky enough to have a Sarah who is naturally gifted at the staff representation game, then can I suggest you pay for whoever is voted by your staff to be their 'leader'/representative to get some training in how to lead a staff forum. It is in your interests, theirs and the staff, and more importantly, really does help to contribute to the overall success of your organisation.

Suggest to your staff that they might like to participate in a staff forum. Explain that it is not a management-controlled exercise, but an opportunity for them to gather together, without management present, to discuss their reactions to what is going on in the organisation and to come up with ideas, suggestions and feedback to the management. However, do make it absolutely clear that the forum is an *addition* to normal communication channels and not a replacement.

How to implement a staff forum

Encourage the staff to appoint a leader for the forum and then work hard with the leader to help them to understand things from the management perspective as well as from the staff one. That way, if they have access to information about what is going on and why they can discuss and share it with the rest of staff from a more informed perspective and the feedback you get will be constructive and helpful, even if occasionally painful!

I must stress again, however, that you need to be *absolutely* clear that the forum is an addition to normal communication channels with their manager and should not be used as a replacement. What you mustn't do is to rely primarily on the forum for your information, otherwise you undermine the ability of your managers to manage.

You cannot control the forum (and indeed, neither should you try) although what you can do is clarify what it is for and make it clear that the staff forum is not for personal attacks.

All-staff meetings

Staff away days have their place, but the fact is that many senior people assume that the business of team building and communication is polished off by getting everyone together once or twice and year and giving them an enjoyable experience.

This is not the case. Teams are built minute by minute, hour by hour, through the daily, weekly and monthly working and practices of your line managers and their teams.

Having said that, I think that it can be very useful to gather everyone together at least once a year. But I do believe that it has to be meaningful. Whilst it might be good fun for people to hang out and play games, at the end of the day you need to ensure that the game playing is in some way genuinely contributing to everyday effectiveness.

'All-staff' days are a good place to look at the working of the organisation as a whole – to ask people what is going well, what is going less well and what can be done about it. They are also a good way of getting other people to interact with one another. And, if your training budget isn't too tight, and the numbers warrant it, you can get everyone to experience some kind of standard training by asking a trainer to deliver a course for you in-house.

But on the whole, my experience tells me that the best use of this type of day is to get people thinking about the future and engaging with them in conversations about where the organisation is going and how it can get there.

For this kind of day to be really effective I think it is worth getting someone external to facilitate it for you. The reality is that you cannot facilitate your own organisation as well as someone from the outside can, because no matter how skilled you are, your audience (i.e. your staff/volunteers) are likely to perceive you as having some kind of hidden agenda (and indeed, you probably do, because you will have your own thoughts about the issues and ideas about what to do). They are more likely to perceive an external person as not having an agenda. This makes it easier for you to participate fully yourself and for them to be more open and participative.

However, this is not always possible, especially if money is tight. In that case, here are some simple ideas to help your all-staff day to be successful:

- Be clear about what you want the outcome of the day to be. Is it to inform, consult, train?
- Make sure eighty per cent of the day consists of people talking to each other or working together on something – avoid long, big plenary sessions where they have to sit and listen.
- Get their feedback on the day. What worked for them? What didn't? What would they like to see next year?

Don't forget – two important things

Staff are often more interested in how the organisation is seen or is doing in the external context than you realise. Don't focus internal communication solely on internal stuff. Give staff the chance to feel proud, excited, cross and engaged about the organisation in its external context.

Volunteers. Volunteers. Volunteers. You need to take as much care about communicating with them as you do with staff. Find an appropriate mechanism and make it work. And remember that for volunteers face-to-face communication is just as important as it is for staff. It's lazy to rely on written communication. And not only that – it doesn't work! If your volunteers are spread about, do shift work and so on, then find a way. There is one if you look hard enough. Even if it means you and/or your managers coming in one evening or weekend to talk to them. It's part of your responsibility. And they are very important!

Confidentiality

This is a good point to talk about that most destructive of words, 'confidentiality'. There can be no such thing as confidentiality in work unless it is about someone's personal life. If you or any of your managers are given a piece of information about a member of staff, a piece of work or whatever, it is your duty to do something about it.

You have to ask yourself, if someone is telling you something in confidence, what exactly is their motive here? Are they trying to get someone else into trouble? Trying to make you think badly of another individual? If people genuinely want a situation resolved then why is 'confidentiality' needed? OK, it may be that they are afraid of being bullied if people find out what they have said, in which case you need to deal with it appropriately and sensitively. But for the most part, I suspect that when people hide behind 'confidentiality' it's because they want to stick the boot in without taking responsibility for it.

So how do you deal with it? Well, to begin with, if someone comes to you and says they want to tell you something in confidence you have to say 'No'. That is, you can't listen to what they have to say in confidence because it is your responsibility as a leader to resolve issues within the organisation. Tell them that if an individual has a problem then you will help them to resolve it. That might involve coaching them so that they go and speak to the individual concerned, or you might step in. Ask people how they would feel if someone told them that another person had a problem with them. The first thing they would want to know is 'Who is this person?'. You can't change anything if you don't know exactly what the problem is and who has it.

I was doing some coaching in an organisation that had a recently appointed chief executive. At a meeting that I was observing the chair told the chief exec that 'some people' had 'some problems' with him. When I asked who had what problems she replied that she couldn't tell me or the chief exec because she had been told in confidence. I pointed out that if the chief exec didn't know who had what problem he could not reasonably be expected to deal with it and therefore the chair could not reasonably expect him to make a judgement about what, if anything, needed to change. So his best course of action was to simply ignore it. All that anonymous, confidential feedback accomplished was to make the chief exec feel undermined and begin to lose confidence – with absolutely no chance of doing anything about it.

My view? Nine times out of ten, it's pure mischief-making. Grown-ups don't send anonymous messages! Don't fall into the trap of encouraging it by paying attention. Make it clear: I will help you to resolve the problem, or I will resolve it for you. If you choose not to resolve it yourself and don't want me to do anything about it either, then that's your choice. But don't expect me to take it seriously in that case. If you do want me to intervene, then remember that I will not be able to keep your identity anonymous – because that is unfair on the individual being criticised. For goodness' sake, our own courts of law do not allow 'accusers' to be anonymous to their accused. How is it that what is absolutely *not* acceptable in civil life is acceptable in work life, particularly when the issues are usually not that serious?

Having said that, you do of course need to bear in mind that bullying and harassment need to be treated somewhat differently (and make sure you have an up-to-date and workable policy to deal with this). In cases of this sort, you may have to be a little more flexible.

Walking the job

When you are at the top of the organisation it is extremely hard to be accessible to the vast majority of your staff, especially if you spend all your time in meetings or at your desk. This is why it is so essential to walk the job. But many chief execs and senior people find this enormously difficult to do. Excuses tend to go something like this:

- They might think I have no work to do if I am just wandering around.
- I don't want to interrupt them at their work.
- I'm too busy.
- It doesn't make any difference to the staff whether I walk the job or not so long as they know I am doing my job.
- It's not a good use of my time.
- Staff will perceive it as meaningless.

The point is you need to be visible – literally. That means that you need to wander about your office/offices so that you can see and be seen.

Why walk the job? Because…

- Staff get used to seeing you around and so are likely to be less intimidated by your job title.
- You can observe things in action for yourself.
- You get the opportunity to ask questions.
- Staff have the chance to 'nobble' you if they have something they want to ask.
- Staff perceive that you are interested in them and their work.

Having said that, walking the job is one of the things that many chief execs tell me they find hardest to do. This is largely because they see it as apparently 'purposeless' and they don't know what to talk about or to say to people. So here are some tips:

- Schedule walk-the-job time in your diary so that you don't forget to do it.
- Do it often, and then you will feel less uncomfortable and so will they.
- Smile and say a general good morning as you walk into the room.
- Look at charts/things on walls, especially if they are tracking progress and ask questions about them.
- Ask what they are working on at the moment.
- If you know something personal, for example, that they have just been on holiday, ask them how it was.
- If you come across something that needs action – then act on it – show that you are paying attention.
- Try to listen more than you talk.
- Don't use it as an opportunity to tell someone off.
- Look for opportunities to 'catch people doing something right!'

Consultation

The greatest compliment that was ever paid to me was when someone asked me what I thought and attended to my answer.

Henry David Thoreau

The above quote sums up for me why it is so important to consult. For one thing, it's useful. You are one brain with one way of looking at the world. Many brains mean many ideas and many ways of looking at the world. There is a very good chance that when you ask people what they think and what their ideas are you will hear things that you didn't expect: fresh ideas; new ways of looking at old problems.

Secondly, nothing makes people feel as valued and important as being asked for their opinions and ideas. It makes them feel part of something more than just their job and that they have the chance to contribute. That alone is likely to make them want to engage more in change and development in the organisation. Even if you can't act on what they suggest, at least you have asked them and they know that you have.

So you can see that consultation with staff and volunteers is vitally important, but is so often done badly. This is because we are not always clear what is and is not up for consultation, or indeed, even what consultation actually is.

Genuine consultation is that which begins *before* you have decided what action to take. That is, you ask people for their input, ideas, feedback and so on before you take any decisions.

There are five stages to consultation:
1 Consult on what the decision(s) should be.
2 Consider what you have heard before making the decision.

3 Make the decision.
4 Communicate the decision and ask for feedback on it if necessary.
5 Check that it is being implemented and is working and amend the decision if
   appropriate.

Do not tell staff you are consulting them if you have already made up your mind.
If you have already decided (and it is entirely right that occasionally you will
make decisions without consulting) then make it clear that you are just informing
them. If you 'pretend' to consult and then don't act on their feedback your
consultation mechanism will lose all credibility – and your ability to get people
to implement your decisions will be undermined.

Generally speaking, when consulting on big decisions, it is better to conduct
consultations face to face around a specific set of questions. For example, if you
are consulting about the cramped conditions in the offices and are aware that an
office move may be required then you might ask questions like:

- What is it about our current conditions that is causing us difficulty?
- What are the possible solutions to the problem?
- What haven't we considered?

This way, you may find that people come up with a solution that you hadn't even
considered. And at the very least you will be able to say genuinely, when you
brief your final decision, that you had listened to staff and taken into account
their views. Then they are more likely to cooperate or even 'own' the decision
that has been taken. But it needs to be genuine. Believe it or not, staff really do
have inbuilt bull**** detectors!

Listening

Talking about consultation (which obviously involves the ability to listen) brings
me on to the issue of listening.

One of the key skills you need as a leader is the ability to listen. It's a funny
thing when you think about it: when we are young we are taught how to read,
how to write and how to speak – but no one actually teaches us how to listen.

> *I wanna be the leader*
> *I wanna be the leader*
> *Can I be the leader?*
> *Can I? I can?*
> *Promise? Promise?*
> *Yippee I'm the leader*
> *I'm the leader*
>
> *OK what shall we do?*

This poem by Roger McGough[3] usually makes people laugh because our normal
concept of leadership (especially at the top) is that the leader knows exactly what

needs to be done and how, and therefore does the deciding. In this poem someone has begged to be the leader but doesn't know what to do.

But actually the poem, for me, is telling about what really powerful leadership is about. It's about asking and listening first before deciding. So 'Now what shall we do?' is a really good question for a leader to ask.

Those of you who have attended coaching or counselling skills courses will, no doubt, have experienced the training that distinguishes between active and passive listening. You will have learned that you need to indicate that you are listening through appropriate body language, using your voice to indicate listening through grunts and 'mmmms'. However, I suspect that if you have to think about doing those things in order to demonstrate that you are listening then you probably aren't genuinely listening at all.

Actually, I don't believe listening is a skill. I believe it's an attitude. When you genuinely want to hear what someone has to say you do pay close attention and listen carefully. So if you want to be an effective listener then the trick is to make yourself want to hear. What makes me want to listen is the fear that I might miss something really important if I don't!

Although, isn't it funny how people think you haven't listened if you haven't agreed? That is why, when you disagree with someone, you need to demonstrate you have listened by being clear about why you don't agree.

Listening is hard in the normal course of things because we have so much going on inside our heads. The trouble is that our thoughts don't switch off when we are listening: we are interpreting what we hear; comparing it with what we already know; thinking of a response. That is normal human behaviour. And in some ways I suspect it's even harder when you are at the top because you have access to so much information which can cause 'interference' when you are listening to others.

Further, the way in which we listen is hugely affected by the filters through which we are hearing the speaker. We listen with the 6 Es: our ears, our eyes, our emotions, our experience, our expectations and our egos. Obviously we hear what people have to say, and not just through their words but also the tone of their voice. We hear with our eyes, in that we observe their body language and thereby add interpretation to the words we are hearing. We also hear with our emotions. If we are feeling negative or cross then that is likely to affect our listening. We have experiences which affect how we hear: we may have a previous, negative experience of an individual which makes it harder for us to listen openly, or we may feel we've 'heard it all before'. We have expectations. We will anticipate what someone is going to say and how they are going to say it because of who they are, or our past experience of them, or what we assume that 'type' of person or person at that job level is likely to say. And finally we listen with our egos. We listen for what makes us feel good about ourselves, or shows us up in a good light.

This is how people will be listening to you all the time. There are only two things that you can do to counteract it. Firstly, recognise that this is what's happening and adjust your speaking accordingly. Secondly, ensure that other people's experience of your listening tells them you are open to hearing them, because that is more likely to encourage similar listening in them.

In terms of your own listening, focus on your attitude and approach to your listening. I do not believe it is possible to listen in a vacuum, to have absolutely no thoughts or reaction to what you are hearing. So I believe the best approach is to focus on your attitude to your listening. Are you:

- Listening 'for being right', i.e. right about them or right about your view?
- Listening 'for punishing', i.e. looking for the mistake or them proving to you how useless they are?
- Listening 'for proving' you know best?
- Listening 'for making' your point?
- Listening 'for telling' your story?
- Listening 'for them being wrong'?

The type of listening that will make us more effective as leaders is:

- Listening 'for understanding' – where are they coming from; why are they saying what they are saying?
- Listening 'for resolution' – what can you do to move things forward?
- Listening 'for action' – what can you do to help?
- Listening 'for possibility' – what new idea is coming out of their words?
- Listening 'for resolving breakdowns' – where can you find agreement?
- Listening 'for building relationships' – where is the common ground?

You won't always listen well. None of us do. But at the very least you can continually ask yourself: are you listening with the right attitude?

Some critical dos and don'ts!

DO	DON'T
■ Have an ear to the gossip ■ Communicate frequently and regularly with staff and volunteers ■ Genuinely consult ■ Communicate primarily through your managers ■ Manage your own behaviour	■ Gossip yourself ■ Rely on all staff/volunteer days to communicate and inspire ■ Consult if you have no intention of changing your mind ■ Assume managers will communicate effectively without training and discussion ■ Allow the way you appear to interfere with what you are trying to do

5 Top teams

If anything goes bad, I did it. If anything goes semi good, we did it. If anything goes really good, you did it. That's all it takes to get people to win football games for you.
Joe Paterno, US football coach

Outcomes

After reading this chapter you will:

- Know how to get your top team to behave more 'corporately'
- Understand some of the underlying dynamics that influence their behaviour
- Have some tips and ideas about how to help them to be a successful top team.

What exactly is a top team?

Of all of the complaints, worries and problems that I encounter, wandering around listening to and working with chief execs in the sector, the issue of the effectiveness of the top team is right there at the top of the list.

And you can see why. You simply cannot do your job alone. You need a top team around you who act corporately, who work well together, who debate and discuss robustly, but who also know when to shut up and get on with it.

Whatever the size of your organisation, your top team is absolutely critical in helping you to achieve the organisation's vision, mission and objectives.

But I wonder. I wonder how much of what you get is what you asked for?

Have you made it clear to the team how incredibly important they are? Have you pointed out to them that this is the team that works with you to provide direction and leadership for the whole organisation? That it is this team that needs to embody the values and culture of the organisation; this team that creates the environment that people work in, that impacts on how staff feel about the organisation, that generates the trust in the leadership and direction of the organisation, and ultimately that enables the organisation to deliver the results that you need.

You know already that a weak link in this team is extremely damaging and limits your ability to achieve. A top team member who is working counter to the rest of the team does two things: they damage trust in the whole leadership of the organisation, which in turn gives rise to credibility issues for the whole team. Secondly, what they do and say reflects on you. People are more inclined to believe those people who are closer to them in 'rank' (for want of a better word) than those who appear far away – so no matter what you say and do yourself, if your message is not being carried down by the rest of your top team then it will not be delivered or believed.

I have noticed that in many organisations the top team is not a top team at all but simply a reporting mechanism. They provide information about progress and results, but do not really engage in a mutual and dynamic conversation about the organisation as a whole, in particular where it is going and how it is going to get there.

Richard Hackman, in his article 'Groups that work and those that don't', defines a real team as one that has '...a collective task that demands a high level of interdependency among its members, something that can only be accomplished together; and clear and stable boundaries so that membership is not constantly changing, and it is easy to tell who is on the team.'

How effective is your top team?

How do you establish what the issues are in your team? How do you know if the team is working well together or not?

In 1998 the Hay Group conducted a study with Harvard and Dartmouth College. This study concluded that the main reason top teams fail is because of the behaviour and actions of the chief executive.

The study looked at how the leadership/managerial style of the chief executive impacted on the ability of the top team to perform. They looked at six dominant leadership styles and assessed that style against the subsequent performance of the team. The styles are:

Coercive – highly directive, forcing people to do things, not involving people in decision making etc.

Authoritative – consulting and listening, but providing clear direction and decisive in action.

Affiliative – involving everyone and focusing on relationships and camaraderie.

Democratic – essentially 'voting', i.e. going with the group majority vote.

Pace-setting – fast moving, focus on action and results.

Coaching – minimal direction, getting people to set their own agendas.

They discovered that in order of effectiveness, in terms of performance of the top team, the styles rank as follows:

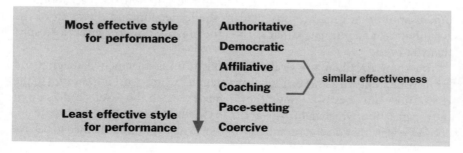

Do you think you are being authoritative when in fact you are being coercive? Are you sure that what you see as being democratic is not simply ducking out of making hard decisions?

I want to pick on this word 'democratic'. And I want to be clear. Voluntary organisations are not democracies. Let me say it again – not democracies. A democracy is one where people vote in their leaders. You didn't get voted in. You were appointed by a board. The same is true for your senior team. You appointed them (or your predecessor did). You cannot run your top team by getting people to 'vote'. That's not to say that you shouldn't involve them, listen to them hard and sometimes do it their way or the majority way – but only because for a particular decision at a particular time that is the right way.

It's important not to polarise completely styles of leading your top team. In the real world, you usually need a combination of them, and the trick is to ensure that you are using the right style at the right time. For example, there will be a time when you need to set the pace – when the need for change is urgent. But constantly operating at full pelt will eventually wear people out. There will be a time when you have to insist that a certain line is taken or that a decision goes a certain way, because the future of the organisation depends on it. But again, this should be rare. The trick is to be aware of what your natural inclination is and ensure that you are actively thinking about what style is appropriate in what circumstances. And if you find that the style you are using is not working – then use a different style. But don't get stuck in only one way of operating.

How do you know if your team is performing?

If your top team is performing well, in addition to seeing results you will also see demonstrated the following behaviours:

- flexibility
- establishing and meeting standards
- co-operation
- empathy
- commitment
- energy.

The following questionnaire can be a helpful starting point for establishing where your team is doing well, and where you need to concentrate your efforts. If the team scores low on one statement, it may be that you need to spend some time and attention there. This questionnaire can be completed by you alone, or by your team together. I use a variation on this a couple of times a year with my own top team. We all complete it and then we look at each statement one by one and share our scores. If there is either a wide discrepancy between members of the team on one particular statement, or if overwhelmingly we score low on one, then we open up the statement for discussion and discuss why people put the scores they did and what we can do about moving the scores upwards.

Generally this works extremely well, particularly as it gives the members of the team an opportunity to raise issues in a non-threatening manner as it is in the context of a more general conversation.

You can, of course, reproduce this self-assessment questionnaire and change the statements to ones that feel more relevant to your organisation. This one is a generalised one to illustrate the example, and the statements are ones that I have discovered reflect common issues at top team level.

High-performing top teams

Self assessment – how well do the following statements describe you?

The team:

1 Has a common understanding of the vision/mission/purpose

Low				Medium					High
1	2	3	4	5	6	7	8	9	10

2 Sees itself as accountable for the whole

Low				Medium					High
1	2	3	4	5	6	7	8	9	10

3 Constantly seeks to improve the organisation

Low				Medium					High
1	2	3	4	5	6	7	8	9	10

4 Focuses on solutions not problems

Low				Medium					High
1	2	3	4	5	6	7	8	9	10

5 Engages in robust and useful debate

Low				Medium					High
1	2	3	4	5	6	7	8	9	10

6 Focuses on strategic and high-level operational issues

Low				Medium					High
1	2	3	4	5	6	7	8	9	10

7 Publicly shows a united front

Low				Medium					High
1	2	3	4	5	6	7	8	9	10

8 Has a high level of empathy and co-operation with one another

Low				Medium					High
1	2	3	4	5	6	7	8	9	10

9 Communicates openly, honestly and appropriately with one another

Low				Medium					High
1	2	3	4	5	6	7	8	9	10

10 Demonstrates trust and loyalty to all fellow members of the leadership team

Low				Medium					High
1	2	3	4	5	6	7	8	9	10

What is the top team's scope and purpose?

The purpose of the top team is to create the conditions for success in future. They do this in two ways: through their 'technical' responsibilities and through their leadership responsibilities.

A member of a top team essentially has two parts to their role, each of which is of equal importance (but interestingly, only one of which is usually monitored!). One is their 'technical' accountability, for example the head of finance is accountable for the finance function, the director of operations is accountable for the operations function, the director of policy is accountable for policy development and so on. The other part of their role is as a leader of the whole organisation. Staff generally do see the top team as being accountable for the whole, even when the team doesn't always behave in that way.

One of the major breakdowns at top level, in my experience, is where the members of the top team have not realised about their wider responsibilities in the corporate context and therefore tend to operate in their own 'silo', that is, focusing on the work of their own bit of the organisation and not taking responsibility for the whole. And yet, this is why they are a member of a top team, precisely because, at their level, delivery in their area is about the contribution to the whole.

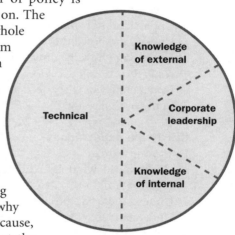

The top team role

Many chief executives find this a real problem at top team level. And often actually the cause of the problem is very simple – no one (the no one being you – the chief exec!) has explained this part of their responsibility to the top team members. There are some who grasp it naturally – but not many – and therefore, if you are a chief executive, it is important that you ensure that your top team understands the entirety of their role – not just the half of it that relates to delivery in their specific area. You can't expect them simply to learn this other part by osmosis, mainly, because in fact it is the hardest part of the job. It needs to be spelled out, monitored, appropriate behaviour rewarded and inappropriate behaviour dealt with.

Clarifying the top team's technical responsibilities is generally very straightforward – members need to deliver on their bit of the organisation's work.

Their leadership responsibilities are a little harder to explain. Simply put, they are usually something like this:

- To participate in robust discussion with the rest of the senior team about the long-term future of the organisation.
- To create a culture in the organisation that is compatible with its ethos and vision.

- To 'own' the leadership message and act as if it was their own.
- To be accountable for the overall performance of the organisation.

How do you achieve their understanding and commitment?

Clarify the context
Does your team:
- Understand and commit to the vision, mission and purpose of the organisation?
- Understand how they fit into the wider context?
- Understand how other members of the team fit into the wider context?
- Understand how the direction and plans for the organisation will deliver the results?
- Understand what they need to do in their technical area in order to contribute to the overall results?

Clarify the expectations
Does your team:
- Understand what is expected of them as someone at the top of the organisation?
- Understand what the culture is that you are trying to create, and buy in to it?
- Understand what the 'leadership' line is of your particular organisation?
- Know what the priorities are?
- Seek solutions, not over-analyse problems?

Clarify the behaviours
Does your team:
- Understand the decision-making process?
- Understand the limits of their authority?
- Understand what are considered appropriate leadership behaviours?
- Hold one another accountable for meeting commitments and deadlines?
- Know how to communicate effectively with one another?

Conditions for success
I have observed that really great top teams appear to have the following things in common.
1 There is a clear compelling direction.
2 The structure is appropriate to the needs of the organisation.
3 The right people are in the right jobs.
4 They are supported by their chief exec and trustees.
5 They are continually developing.

So how do you make sure these ingredients are in place?

Establish a clear compelling direction

This sounds self-evident, but does your team really understand the overall direction of the organisation?

- Don't assume they know the direction.
- Articulate it for them.
- If you can't get agreement, get alignment.

Get the structure right

This is not so much the organisational structure, but the structure of communication and responsibility within the team itself:

- Establish norms and enforce them.
- Create 'rules' for how your top team meetings are run.
- Establish how you expect people to interact with one another.
- Clarify the decision-making structure and ensure that at any decision point, it is clear what the actual decision is about, what kind of decision it is (i.e. consensus, collegiate, consulted) and who is going to take it.

Get the right people

Easier said than done! And very often you inherit people who you have to work with. Nonetheless, if the people you inherit aren't working with you then you have to surround yourself with people who are. Not 'yes' men or women. But people who are enthusiastic, engaged and who challenge you even as they're working alongside you.

Here my advice is, given a choice between those people who are highly technically competent and those people who have the right 'attitude', I would tend to choose the latter. This is because it is relatively easy to train people in the skills and knowledge they need to do the job; it is almost impossible to train people in the right attitude.

Look for someone who:

- has a high degree of emotional intelligence;
- has enthusiasm and energy for the job;
- demonstrates empathy for others;
- demonstrates integrity;
- has the ability to challenge the team to live up to its values;
- has the ability to engage in productive conflict;
- openly says what they are thinking;
- walks the talk – i.e. matches behaviour to words;
- can speak for those who are not present without putting their own particular 'spin' on it.

Support them

What does this actually mean? Well, I think it's about the following:

- allowing them to make mistakes without getting into 'trouble';

- talking through with them what they are doing – but allowing them to make their own decisions;
- backing them up when they get it wrong;
- praising them publicly when they get it right.

Develop them

Don't assume that they know how to do all the things that are expected of them at the top of the organisation. If you don't want them to learn the hard way (and make life difficult for you and their people along the way!) you must ensure that they participate in learning and development activities such as:

- facilitated planning days
- leadership training
- work shadowing
- having a dedicated coach (a professionally qualified one who you pay for).

Group dynamics

You need to have a basic understanding of what is going on at the group dynamic level in order to be able to know how to deal appropriately with some of the (frankly often bizarre!) behaviour you see at the top of the organisation.

It is my observation that the nearer people get to the top, the more often you see examples of childlike (even childish) behaviours. Why is this?

Well, if you think about the standard model of an organisation in the voluntary sector it probably looks something like this:

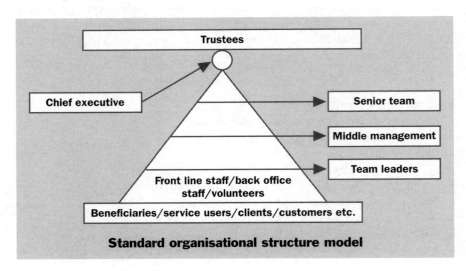

Standard organisational structure model

You may have more or fewer layers in between you and the front line staff, but essentially there is a clear linear structure. Now, if you turn that structure around to represent what really happens in an organisation in terms of the 'weight' of responsibility it looks something like this:

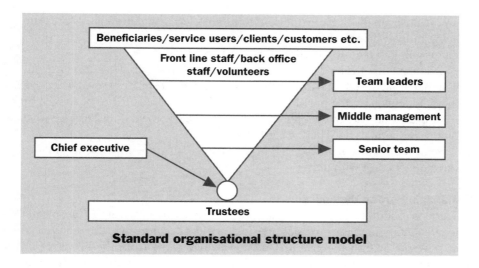

Beneficiaries/service users/clients/customers etc.	
Front line staff/back office staff/volunteers	Team leaders
	Middle management
Chief executive	Senior team
Trustees	

Standard organisational structure model

(Incidentally, this reverse organisational model I call the 'leader-as-servant' model. It is supposed to demonstrate that our role as leaders is to support the rest of the organisation so that they can serve our end-users, rather than the other way around. It is a powerful model and I think very effective – why not share the concept with your team?)

In this model you can see that service users/ beneficiaries and so on have a broad base of support – from the front line/back office staff/volunteers, who in turn have a base of support in their team leaders, who have middle management; and all of whom are leaning on the senior team for support.

So you can see that, in fact, all other parts of the organisation have a relatively broad base of support, that is, more than one person to 'lean' on – including you, as you have the trustees (theoretically!) for support. But all the senior team have is one person – you. If you can visualise them literally standing on you, you might get a picture of how unstable and insecure it can feel. One member of your team may feel they have both feet firmly planted in the middle of your back – they feel secure, stable and supported by you. But that doesn't leave a lot of room for the others. There may be one who, metaphorically speaking, feels they are balancing

precariously on the heel of your right foot! They feel unstable and insecure. And being human beings, if they feel unstable and insecure, some way or another that is going to manifest itself in their behaviours.

On top of this, the level of expectation of them is very high. They are conscious that they are at the top, and, particularly for those who are relatively inexperienced, they suddenly have the horrible realisation that they are going to be judged by what others do (i.e. the people in their teams/departments) and not by what they as individuals do. That's a hard place to be.

So how does this manifest itself in your team and, more importantly, how on earth do you deal with it?

Managing group dynamics
There is a body of research which indicates that when a group of people get together, there is an unconscious pressure on them to conform to those perceived as powerful within the group. This power may come from the power of an individual (i.e. someone seen as being more credible, charismatic, capable, more experienced etc. than someone else) or the power of the majority. Not all members of the group will conform, but the critical point for you is that once a majority 'gang' up it is more difficult for them to evaluate objectively or to consider the 'contrary evidence', namely that evidence which does not support the group's view. This is dangerous, because the fact is that the most powerful individual is often not right. And the majority view is not always the right view – simply the most commonly held one. Further, ganging up also runs the risk of isolating the member of the team who has not given in to the group pressure.

To resolve this problem try the following:
- Clarify the task – check the team's understanding of the facts and the end point, discuss consequences and risks, and look at alternative routes.
- Clarify the group structure – accountabilities and authorities, so that if, for example, the director of fundraising wants to take a particular route in fundraising strategy which the rest of the team does not support, then emphasise to the team that it is, nonetheless, the decision of the director of fundraising even if the rest of the team do not agree – and that it is their job to support that individual.
- Allow individuals to express their differences openly, without allowing one particular 'position' to be seen to be 'rewarded'.
- Acknowledge the need for social approval.
- Establish agreements by asking individuals to verbalise their thoughts.
- Identify and illuminate in-groups and out-groups – point out openly where you see 'gangs' or 'cliques' forming or where you see that one particular view is not gaining an appropriate hearing.

Human beings are gregarious folk, who want to find people that they can identify with, who they perceive as sharing their values. They essentially seek 'like' others.

In any organisation there are in-groups and out-groups which share common characteristics. This is normal, but creates the possibility that an entire group could be discredited or discounted because they are not part of the in-group. For example, a classic divide in the voluntary sector is between those in fundraising and those in finance – with both teams stereotyping and labelling the others, and having a perception and expectation of the behaviours of the other group, which they subsequently actively seek evidence to support.

To resolve this issue try the following:
- Illuminate the group stereotype – expose it and discuss it.
- Challenge the stereotypes – seek contrary evidence.
- Acknowledge, encourage and praise differences in opinion/approach.
- Accept and understand the need people have to identify with a group – but encourage open discussion.
- Base questions along the lines of:
  - Tell me more about…?
  - What do you think about…?
  - How do you feel about…?
  - What will you accept as evidence?
  - What information are we missing?
  - What counter arguments can you think of?
  - What are the pros/cons?
  - What are the consequences if we do…if we don't…?

People's willingness to adopt certain positions or support certain decisions will be highly influenced by what they perceive to be in and out-groups, whether they perceive those groups to be like or unlike them, and where they see themselves in relation to those groups.

A simple analogy is that of a group of people, men and women, some of whom are parents and some of whom aren't. Within that group there will be mothers – who are likely to perceive all other mothers as being similar to themselves, so they are likely to feel the need to have common agreement with their similar in-group. Fathers will perceive themselves as being in the in-group (because they have the common bond of children) but dissimilar to it (because they are a different sex). The out-group will be those people who are not parents. The similar out-group will be women who are not parents (who share a sex, hence the perception of similarity, but not the role of parent – therefore not in the in-group) and the dissimilar out-group will be men who are not parents (who are a different sex and are not parents so will see nothing in common between them and the in-group).

If the similar in-group of mothers is the 'lead' or most dominant force then you are likely to find that most of the other mothers will support that group view, that the fathers are more likely to go along with the group norm than the female non-parents who, nonetheless, may go along with the group because they can see some similarities between them and the in-group, even though they are not part of it. And the male non-parents are highly unlikely to conform to the norm of the female parents (i.e. mothers) in-group because they perceive they have nothing in common.

Critically, this means that people will evaluate the *source* of a piece of information as being of more importance than the information itself. If it comes from a member of a similar in-group it will be given more validity by those members of that in-group than if it comes from a group perceived as dissimilar and out.

This is illustrated in the following diagram.

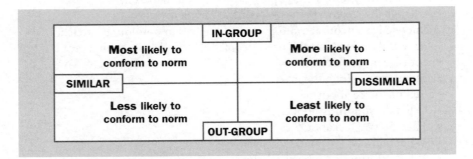

The point here is that you don't want decisions or positions to be influenced primarily by this in and out-group dynamic – you want them to be influenced by the facts of the matter. To resolve this try the following:

- Focus discussions on outcomes, not method.
- Question discrepancy between original individual judgements and movement.
- Agree values around how information will be received and evaluated.
- Seek contrary evidence.
- Take into account out-group views.

Sub-conscious group behaviours

Essentially, as an adult we demonstrate behaviours which we learned as children in constructing defences to deal with sub-conscious anxiety, anxiety that we are not necessarily aware that we are feeling.

There are three classic symptoms (for want of a better word) of this anxiety-avoidance pressure.

- Denial – not acknowledging our own feelings and often 'projecting' these feelings on to others.
- Projection – benign and malign (i.e. hero-ising or demonising others).
- Scape-goating – group projection on to an individual.

I observed a real instance of these subconscious processes in action. I worked with an organisation that went through an intensive and extreme restructure. They began with around 40 members of the senior team (it was a large organisation). The new structure had only 20 senior team roles. So, consequently, half of the previous senior team was either effectively demoted or made redundant. The other half was given brand new roles. In this process, a more junior member of staff was unexpectedly (to her and the rest of the senior team) promoted to one of the new senior roles (let's call her Grace). So she was new to the team and to the level of responsibility – and she was *the only one* in this situation. For the rest of the new team, they already had experience at that level, they all knew each other and, further, they were, naturally, very attached to their colleagues who had not 'made the grade' so to speak.

As a result of all of this, Grace entered a team of highly emotionally charged people who were feeling a curious mixture of guilt, sorrow and shame because they were 'in' and the others were 'out', but who also felt pride and excitement in their new roles and wanted to demonstrate that they were a good and right choice in the new structure.

Grace was naïve and completely oblivious to these feelings and leapt in full of enthusiasm, energy and ideas, combined with inexperience and a skewed understanding of what leadership was about at that level.

The team were unable to deal with their feelings of anxiety and this was not acknowledged or dealt with by the leadership of the organisation. There was no time given to grieve, no guidance given on how to deal with these conflicting and difficult emotions, either to the team itself or to Grace. The organisation, again, understandably, wanted the new team to just get on with the job. So these feelings remained unresolved.

The result was that Grace was effectively scape-goated. For a period of at least a year, her ideas were dismissed, her credibility was questioned, her skills were denigrated (or at least that's how it felt to her and I could see from observing that some of this was indeed happening – although perhaps not to the extreme that she perceived it). It was clear to me, by the time I became involved, that what was happening was a classic example of group psychodynamic defence mechanisms: a combination of denial, projection and scape-goating enabled the team to function, if not wonderfully, at least enough to survive.

This story, whilst true, is probably an extreme example of these processes in action. Nonetheless, they may well be in action in your own team, so it is worth observing what is happening within it.

To resolve issues of this kind try the following:
- Encourage and allow the group to express anxiety.
- Challenge individuals who 'speak on behalf of…' or use the term 'people'.
- Ask direct questions – how do you personally feel?
- Ask for the source of the feeling/perception.
- Evaluate the evidence.
- Establish a set of agreed values and associated behaviours – review them regularly.

How do you get the team to think and act 'corporately'?

This is indeed a challenge. I would begin by agreeing with the team a set of leadership 'standards' to which you all sign up. Get it written down and then get into the habit of reviewing how well you are doing against these values on a regular basis. At DSC, we review these values and standards on a regular basis, in fact it is usually the first item on every senior management team meeting agenda.

One of the mechanisms you have for working with your senior team is your regular meeting. You will determine what 'regular' is depending on the size of your organisation. But it is important that these meetings are diarised in and the time, date and place of this meeting should be scheduled a whole year in advance, so that the team knows when it is and can organise its work around it.

Also, beware of the meeting simply being a catch-up or reporting mechanism. The bulk of this meeting probably ought to be future focused.

Have a properly set out agenda, prepared in advance, which makes it clear who is expected to speak on what topic, at what length and with what expected outcome. Then stick to it!

At your meeting make sure that you clarify both on the agenda and at the start of each agenda item the following:
- The expected outcome of discussion:
  - information?
  - decision?
  - consultation?
- What type of decision it is:
  - consensus – the majority
  - collegiate – building it together
  - owned – an individual.

And at the end of each agenda item or the meeting as a whole clarify what the management 'line' will be, namely that we are all behind this decision in public, even if we disagreed privately. And make it clear that you will not tolerate your senior team ignoring the management line.

Managing team conflicts

You need to recognise that disagreement is an essential part of team work. If a team does not have strong feelings and emotions but relies simply on facts to make its decisions it is effectively a less intelligent team (see Daniel Goleman's excellent work on emotional intelligence for more about this). The best decision makers use both facts and feelings.

To begin with, unproductive conflict usually happens because it has not been made clear what the decision-making process is and who is responsible for specific decisions.

You need to clarify the distinction between responsibility, authority and accountability. Responsibility is for us all. We are responsible for the whole whether it is in our area or not. Authority is for the specific manager – who has the authority to make decisions about their bit of the business and at what level. And accountability is for their specific job and area. They are accountable for ensuring that their bit delivers.

Once that's cleared up you then need to make sure that people understand what type of decision is being made. Is it consensus (i.e. we all have to agree), autocratic (only the decision of the accountable person) or collegiate (worked out together)? All three of these decision-making strategies are acceptable. The trick is to know which one you need.

Be clear on these questions:
- Whose decision is it?
- At what point can the challenge stop?
- What do you do if you really disagree with the decision and can't support it?
- What are you looking for – agreement, alignment, acceptance?

My experience is that it is better to seek alignment than acceptance. If you ask someone to accept a decision that they don't agree with, you are effectively asking them to admit that they are wrong – and that is very hard to do, especially if they don't believe they are. If you ask them to align with it, you are making the point that you have heard that they don't agree, but that in the interests of moving forward can they position themselves behind the decision and support its implementation (i.e. align). Much easier for people to do!

If, however, conflict is still rearing its head and you are finding it hard to manage you could try some of the following actions:

Build a positive approach
- Explain that conflict is normal.
- Encourage the team to understand that conflict is healthy if handled well.
- Don't try to stifle or 'control' disagreement – concentrate on encouraging individuals to listen to others' points of view.

Clarify expectations
- Is the team clear what its purpose is?
- Do you have ground rules governing behaviours?
- Have you talked about how to depersonalise conflict?
- Is everyone clear about the level of authority/decision-making/accountability of others within the team?
- Do you have a structured way of dealing with discussions?
- Are performance expectations clearly defined and understood by everyone?

Identify the type of conflict
- Is it personal to the individual?
- Is it conflict between individuals?
- Is it conflict with the whole team?
- Is it conflict between several individuals?
- Is it conflict with someone or a group outside the team?

Identify the team needs
- Situation – what is the problem to be solved?
- Options – what are the possible solutions?
- Long-term consequences – what would resolve the problem?
- Victory – what would a positive result look like?
- Execute – carry out the actions required.

Depersonalise the conflict
Create the environment for a solution by getting the team to address the following:
- What happened/is happening?
- What were/are the consequences (facts and feelings)?
- What would/will it take to move on?

Structure the discussion
- Let each person have their say.
- Engage neutral team members to reflect on areas of agreement and disagreement.
- Explore areas of disagreement to identify specific issues.
- Have opponents suggest modifications to their own points of view as well as to those of others.
- If you can't get agreement, go for alignment.

Key questions for resolving conflict
- What are we trying to accomplish as a team?
- What are each of our roles and responsibilities in accomplishing our goals?
- Do we have the 'who' and 'when' and 'what' information?
- If we get into trouble who can help us?
- How will we arrive at decisions?
- What strengths do we bring to establishing our goals?
- How do we make ourselves more accessible to each other?
- What are we doing that is blocking resolution to this problem?
- How can we express differences without blaming others?
- What behaviours are unproductive? How can we help individuals to take ownership of their behaviour? Don't excuse a team member when they behave badly.

Some critical dos and don'ts!

DO	DON'T
■ Make sure your top team members understand their wider leadership responsibilities ■ Be aware of the group dynamics underlying their behaviour ■ Agree a set of leadership standards ■ Have regular diarised meetings ■ Allow healthy conflict to manifest itself	■ Try to take their decisions for them ■ Forget how vulnerable they feel ■ Forget to hold them to the standards ■ Focus on the operation at the expense of the strategic ■ Forget to clarify whose decision it is

6 Trusting trustees

My grandfather once told me that there were two kinds of people: those who do the work and those who take the credit. He told me to try to be in the first group; there was much less competition.

Indira Gandhi, first woman Prime Minister of India

Outcomes:

After reading this chapter you will:
- **Have some ideas about how to deal with your more 'challenging' trustees**
- **Have a better understanding of what motivates them**
- **Be aware of some of the things you might do that make it harder for you.**

In this chapter I speak both as a chief exec and as a trustee of another charity. So I am taking into account both 'sides' of the story as I look at the relationship between chief exec/senior team and trustees.

What is the role of the chief exec in relation to the board?

The nature and involvement of trustees in the running of a voluntary organisation is highly dependent upon the size, age and make-up of the organisation concerned. Smaller organisations with fewer staff will probably find that their trustees are more involved than those that are slightly larger.

There is much talk about what is the 'right' role of the trustees in respect of the difference between governance and leadership. My view is that this grey area is flexible and shifting. There will be times when trustees either need to be or want to be heavily involved and other times when they want you just to get on with it. You need to develop the ability to respond appropriately to both situations.

You also need to accept the fact that your 'bosses' are effectively part-time volunteers who will often know less about your organisation than you and your staff – and I know that many chief execs and senior staff find this very frustrating. But never forget what a truly effective system of governance this can be. Disregarding personalities for the moment, it is precisely because they are often not involved in the day-to-day running of the organisation that they are more able to avoid getting side-tracked by how things are done, especially if you encourage them to think strategically.

Further, and importantly, if you cannot afford to employ the level of experienced staff that your organisation needs, you can compensate with that by ensuring you have specialist, experienced board members who can supply knowledge that you don't have and who give expert advice.

Don't forget that your board members are often deeply committed to the values and cause of the organisation. If you make the effort to work alongside them, to be supportive and understanding, you will have valuable advisers, advocates and supporters.

If your board is not having the kind of discussions or engagement with the organisation that facilitates its development, then you need first to look to yourself and your input to that process. The fact is that a good board is as much about how hard you work at it as it is about the board itself.

Although you are not part of the board, your role is absolutely critical in keeping members informed and helping them to make the right kinds of decisions and interventions at the right sort of time.

I was working alongside a chief exec who was having real issues with his board. They were constantly interfering in the running of the organisation and he was enormously frustrated because he felt that they were challenging his leadership of the organisation. The big issue was one of direction. The board and he disagreed about the right route for the organisation to take. He felt the organisation's best hope for the future was to work more closely with the local authority. His board were absolutely determined to remain independent of what they perceived to be a form of 'government influence' on their work.

He found it deeply irritating that they weren't agreeing with him. There were two things we needed to work on. The first concerned his approach, which wasn't very helpful. He wasn't using the right sort of language or tone in order to get his message across. The second was the real problem – he had forgotten that it is absolutely the right, even the responsibility, of the board to determine the long-term direction of the charity. I think we, as chief execs, forget that at our peril. We are the implementers. That doesn't mean that we don't have an enormous impact or important role to play on the long-term future of the organisation, but ultimately that is what trustees are there for. In the end, the chief exec left.

Your job is essentially to advise, inform and deliver. You are the appointed officer of the board. You need to listen to their views and share your own. Although you are not technically a member of the board, nonetheless, you should establish a relationship with them so that at board meetings the sense is one of partnership between you and them, that you are working together towards the same goal.

If you get this right, you and your board will have a dynamic, sometimes frustrating, but ultimately rewarding and successful relationship which enables you and them to lead a powerful and successful organisation.

Make up of the board

The make up and constitution of your board of trustees is only dependent upon your governing documents. And contrary to popular opinion, these can be changed relatively easily. If your board is not working well because its governing documents don't allow it to, then change them.

Ask your board to answer the following questions:

- Do our governance documents reflect the reality of the world we are currently in?
- What do our objects allow us to do and not to do? Do we need to change them in order to move in a new direction?
- Do our governance documents allow us the freedom to develop in new ways in response to future opportunities?
- Do we have the right make up of board members?
- Do we have the right number of trustees? Should we have more/less?
- Do we have the right length of service for trustees?

Having this conversation will help them to think about their purpose as well as to ensure that your governance is fit for the future.

Is your board effective? Does it know what it needs to do? Get your trustees to complete the following questionnaire so that they can discuss what works and what doesn't and focus on what can be done. If these generic questions aren't right for your board, change the questionnaire and put in more appropriate ones.

Boards – good governance

Self Assessment – how well do the following statements describe the performance of the board?

1 The board has a common understanding of the vision/mission/values and strategic objectives

Low				Medium					High
1	2	3	4	5	6	7	8	9	10

2 The board focuses on strategic issues

Low				Medium					High
1	2	3	4	5	6	7	8	9	10

3 The board delegates appropriate authority to the executive team

Low				Medium					High
1	2	3	4	5	6	7	8	9	10

4 The board allows the management of the charity to be carried out by the executive team, without undue interference

Low				Medium					High
1	2	3	4	5	6	7	8	9	10

5 The board is diverse and representative of the community and people the charity serves

Low				Medium					High
1	2	3	4	5	6	7	8	9	10

6   The board regularly reviews its own performance

Low				Medium					High
1	2	3	4	5	6	7	8	9	10

7   The board has an open, fair and appropriate recruitment and selection policy for new trustees

Low				Medium					High
1	2	3	4	5	6	7	8	9	10

8   The board sets clear terms of reference for sub-committees

Low				Medium					High
1	2	3	4	5	6	7	8	9	10

9   The board fully understands its obligations in terms of compliance with its own governing documents and relevant legislation

Low				Medium					High
1	2	3	4	5	6	7	8	9	10

10 The board encourages all stakeholders in the charity's planning and decision-making

Low				Medium					High
1	2	3	4	5	6	7	8	9	10

Why do people become trustees?

From observing and working with a number of trustees in various different capacities I notice a number of things about their motivation to become a trustee.

There are those who simply feel passionately about the cause of the charity and want to get involved. Then there are those who have fully contributed during their professional lives, often in some completely different field, and feel the need to give back to society in some way. As they are very often senior in background, their preferred route is governance rather than practical work. You rarely find ex-company directors dishing out the tea or driving the mini-bus. For some, that is because they realise that their experience may be more useful at board level, but for others it relates to status. Often, if they are retired, they have a sense of loss for that status. This is absolutely not a criticism. It is a completely normal human reaction and one which we simply need to recognise. Some trustees seek to support a charity that has a cause close to their hearts – others don't particularly mind which charity. Some become a trustee because they believe it will enhance their reputation in their community or look good on a CV. And for some, it is because they think the organisation is being run badly and that they will be able to improve things.

The important point to note about the motives is that, actually, they don't matter all that much. What matters is that the individual is bringing to your board something that the board doesn't already have – in terms of background, expertise, skill, knowledge or value base.

The human side of trustees

It can be very hard when you are working with trustees not to get irritated when they expose their human side – when it appears that their egos are getting in the way of you doing your job; when they are more caught up with their relationships with each other or the way the board operates than they are in the work of the charity; when they are concentrating more on the detailed running of the organisation and not enough on their responsibilities as a board; or when they simply don't get on with each other and you feel like 'piggy in the middle'.

This happens in all charities at some point or another. Even if your board is generally extremely good, the chances are that at some stage things will become difficult. This is because they are people, and have exactly the same issues as everyone else.

I have found that there are some common situations that senior people encounter when dealing with trustees.

- They are elected by each other – this often means that they appoint people who are 'like' them and so it can sometimes be hard to get the board to see a different possibility or accept a view that doesn't square with its value set.
- It is common to find a board of trustees with people from very similar backgrounds, education and professional status who bear very little resemblance to the service users or beneficiaries the charity is serving. Whilst it is helpful to have professional expertise, sometimes that brings with it a lack of understanding about the impact of what they do; and an undue interference in the day-to-day running of the organisation.
- Sometimes, the board is so completely different in its make up that it is hard to stop them fighting and agree on a course of action.
- Because it is a voluntary role, it can be challenging to get them to understand fully their duties and to engage appropriately with the charity.

So where to begin in working with them? I advise thinking of them first and foremost as human beings who have needs. Their needs are the same as everyone else's. They want to feel they are doing a good job, that they are valued and appreciated, that they are making a difference, that they are cared for and about, that they are more than simply someone doing a job, and that their colleagues (i.e. other members of the board) like and trust them – exactly the same emotions that your staff and other volunteers have about their role in work.

Some of them will of course deny this and insist that they don't care about their personal needs and that it is all for the greater good of the charity. But you and I know that is not always the case. And neither does it need to be.

There are many trustees who are genuinely very, very good. I have quite a few of them on my board at DSC. The problem is how to deal with those trustees who just 'feel' difficult to deal with.

To begin with you need to ask yourself: is the problem here only about your *perception* of them? If you cast your mind back to the leadership styles questionnaire, are you sure that the differences between you are really fundamental, or simply due to the fact that you work in different ways and have forgotten to make allowances?

Having said that, in the following table I exaggerate the behaviours of some of those trustee types who seem to cause most angst for chief execs and senior staff, for ease of illustration some of the things that you can do to manage them. Your job is as much about managing 'upwards' as it is about managing 'downwards'.

Some examples of difficult behaviours of trustees and how to handle them

Type	Type of behaviour	How to handle it
The know-it-all	This is the person who believes that they know the best way of dealing with every situation – they often appear to be frustrated during the meetings at what they see as the ignorance of their colleagues and particularly the executive team	■ Acknowledge their points – don't argue ■ Ask them to clarify precisely what they mean ■ Remind them of progress to date ■ Ask for their ideas and suggestions ■ Ask for examples of what they believe works
The frustrated chief exec	This is the person who thinks they could do a better job of running the charity than the chief exec – they will frequently offer unwanted advice about matters that are not for them to deal with. They will often interfere with minutiae or tell the chief exec/senior team exactly how to carry out a particular task or duty	■ Ask for their views and opinions ■ Acknowledge their points and say that you will take them into account ■ Don't rise to the bait and get defensive ■ Remind the board often about what is strategic and what is operational by using the appropriate language
The naysayer	This is the person who objects to anything new being proposed	■ Ask them to explain their objection ■ Ask them if they have an alternative suggestion ■ Ask them to consider the pros and cons of action vs inaction
The critic	This is the person who will look for fault or examples of where things have gone badly or where mistakes have been made – they will seek to apportion blame.	■ Listen and don't react ■ Openly acknowledge mistakes – get in there first! ■ Focus on the future and solutions

The 'duty' attendee	This is the person who turns up at meetings and never contributes much to the discussions – you are never sure what their view is	▪ Ask them directly what they think about a particular point (e.g. John, I am interested in your view on this) ▪ Ask them in advance to contribute to a particular agenda item
The absentee	This is the person who turns up occasionally and rarely engages with the Charity in any other way than attending the occasional meeting	▪ Highlight this to your chair and ask her/him to deal with it ▪ Find out what the problem is – do they need some support to attend? ▪ Have a register and share it regularly at board meetings ▪ Publicly thank and acknowledge those who do attend
The historian	This is the person who has usually been around for a long time and is constantly harping back to the past	▪ Honour the past ▪ Acknowledge where the charity has come from and what it has achieved ▪ Talk about the need to ensure that the Charity is fit for the future ▪ Use their historical references to springboard to the current situation/future focus
The volunteer	This is the person who constantly reminds you that they are a volunteer – they will often complain that too much is being asked of them	▪ Grit your teeth! ▪ Ask them what they think is reasonable in terms of their time commitment ▪ Don't ask them to do more than they are prepared to do
The politician	This is the person who has little interest in the workings of the charity but has a lot to say about its role in the wider context	▪ Dedicate space for this kind of topic on the agenda ▪ Remind all trustees regularly that they are **all** accountable for the whole organisation ▪ Honour the usefulness of this input – keeps the organisation thinking beyond operational issues

Relationship with the board

Boards differ from the chief exec in one crucial aspect – they are part of a team of peers – so a sense of 'team-ness' will often be very important to them. The truth is, as the chief exec you are the only one in any organisational structure who is completely alone. You are not part of the team of the board. You are there to advise and inform. It is right and proper that the board should want some time alone to build up their own relationships. The danger is when this gets out of control and they end up making decisions without involving you.

For many boards, the relationship with the chief executive and senior team can be a very frustrating one. They know, deep in their hearts, that you have more influence on what happens to and in the organisation than they do. They know that they can't make you do anything, and that if they force you to do something you don't agree with, you can easily find a way to prove them wrong by ensuring it doesn't work. And even if that is genuinely not what you have done, sometimes it will be perceived that way. Most switched-on boards will realise that the real power base is you and your senior team and that they need to get you on-side in order to achieve what they want to achieve.

You need to be very sensitive to this. And don't abuse it. I have seen rather too many chief executives completely ignore the wishes of the board and go their own route, and the board, particularly if it is not a strong one, feels powerless to do anything about it.

To ensure that the relationship is as positive as it can be there are a number of things you can do.

1 Have the conversation about clarifying what their expectations are of you and your senior team and what your expectations are of them.
2 Agree what is reasonable in terms of preparation for board meetings (i.e. what requires paperwork in advance and what doesn't – and what to do if an issue crops up on which you don't have time to prepare a paper).
3 Ensure that you have an agenda, agreed in advance with your chair, which specifies each agenda item, the nature of the discussion and how long each item will take.
4 Minute your meetings against agenda items so that trustees find it easier to keep track.
5 Keep them updated on progress regularly – even outside normal board meetings.
6 Try to avoid surprising them – particularly with bad news! (Having said that, sometimes you will be accused of surprising them when actually you didn't know either! This is the point at which you simply grit your teeth and acknowledge their worry.)

What should you ask of them?
- To turn up to meetings on time and to stay to the end.
- To read the paperwork in advance of the meeting and to make notes in advance of their questions.
- To tell you in advance if there is a problem/issue they want to raise at the meeting so that you can prepare for it.

- To discuss openly and honestly with you any issues they may have with your leadership of the organisation.
- To involve you in all their decision-making.
- To chastise you in private and support you in public.
- To remember that *you* can never take credit for good performance because as an effective leader your job is to apportion credit and absorb blame – but that success in any area does have a lot to do with your leadership.

What you should not expect

- They will not remember things between meetings – usually they have other work/ jobs/interests which is the primary focus for them and it is not reasonable for you to expect that they will always remember what you have told them before.
- They will not always act as one – they will frequently disagree with one another – and this is not necessarily an example of board disunity. Disagreement is healthy if handled well.
- They will not think that you are the best thing since sliced bread – they are very aware that your performance reflects on them and so they are more likely to be critical than not. That's fair enough and you need to learn not to take it personally.
- They will not always agree that you know what is best for the organisation, indeed they will believe that they are the ones who should know, and so they should.
- Not all of them will trust or respect you – you need only to make sure that the majority do, and concentrate on them. Don't waste time trying to win over a trustee who isn't 'winoverable'! Let your chair deal with them.

Common mistakes made by chief execs in dealing with the board

- Giving too much detailed information.
- Board not given sufficient time to digest information prior to the meeting.
- Reacting to comments/observations made during the meeting without taking time to think and respond appropriately.
- Being defensive when challenged.
- Expecting trustees to understand fully the workings of the organisation.
- Surprises.
- Not listening to board members' suggestions.
- Explaining at great length why their ideas won't work!
- Not respecting their experience/background/skills/history.
- Not taking them seriously.
- Forgetting that they are the ultimate leaders of the organisation.

Your relationship with your chair

It is undoubtedly true that you need to build up a strong relationship with your chair, one that is mutually open and honest. This is hard to do. I have often seen how the chief exec will talk openly about what they are getting wrong, but find that their chair does not do likewise! However, for much the same reasons that you probably don't reveal your internal struggles to your own senior team, your chair will want you to see them as wise, knowledgeable and able to support you in your work.

You need to remember however, that you don't actually report to the chair. The chair acts as a stand-in for the board, for practical and pragmatic reasons. Ultimately you report to the *whole* board and they are all accountable for your performance. So you mustn't let your relationship with your chair become so close that you effectively exclude the rest of the board, otherwise you will both find it difficult to carry out your respective roles.

There is also always the danger that the other trustees will see you and your chair as being 'in cahoots' and therefore an atmosphere of distrust may build up.

I have an excellent chair at DSC. What makes her good? Well, she definitely isn't perfect, but admits to her mistakes. She sees her role as leading the board and mine as leading the staff and our joint responsibility as working with trustees and the staff to lead the whole organisation.

She has only once ever berated me in public (she is a human being and I had driven her nuts!). Otherwise she is as likely to praise and thank as she is to advise or criticise. She respects my judgement and expects me to respect hers. She allows me to make my own mistakes and doesn't say 'I told you so' if I have done it my way, when in hindsight hers would have been better.

She insists that the board supports me and my team in public and deals with any issues privately. She works hard to keep the board involved and communicated with. When we have a one-to-one she usually sends a short e-mail to the rest of the board summarising what we talked about. She concentrates on making sure that the board is delivering on its 'side of the bargain' while freeing me up to deliver on mine. And I'm not telling you her name because you can't have her. She's mine I tell you – mine!

However, much of the reason why she is good is because we agreed, right at the very beginning, what our relationship should be. We clarified the distinction between her role as the Chair of the Board and mine as Chief Executive. We agreed how we would handle things if our relationship got difficult or broke down in some way. And the mere fact of having that conversation has made the subsequent relationship better for the organisation.

We do fall out. We do disagree. We do get cross and frustrated with each another. But we work consciously and hard at getting it right. Do you?

Some critical dos and don'ts!

DO

- Encourage your board to recruit openly for trustees
- Remember your board is made up of human beings too
- Take control by adjusting the way you react to your board
- Make use of their skill and expertise
- Help them to concentrate on strategic issues by using the appropriate language

DON'T

- Allow them to accept as a new trustee someone who already has too many other trusteeships
- Forget to listen to their advice
- Forget they are only part-time and volunteers
- Get cross when they get it wrong
- Give them too much detailed operational information if it's not appropriate

7 Survival isn't mandatory

You don't have to change. Survival isn't mandatory. W Deming

Outcomes

After reading this chapter you will:
- Be clear about why organisations need to change
- Be sensitive to why people resist change
- Have some ideas about how to implement change.

This chapter is about why organisations need constantly to change, how to engage your organisation in change and why one of your most fundamental jobs as a leader at the top of the organisation is to create change, even if the organisation apparently doesn't need to.

Why change?

Actually, this isn't such a daft question as it sounds. Your organisation is doing a good job. You have tried and tested methods of achieving your objectives which are still working. You are managing to attract the sort of funding that you need in order to continue with your work. And you've been around a long time. So why on earth would you change?

Well, the problem is that the world around us is constantly changing, whether we like it or not. And even if fundamental problems don't necessarily change (there are still the poor, the sick, the socially disadvantaged, natural disasters etc.), the way in which those problems manifest themselves and the expectations of the people affected by those problems change. If we are not constantly looking to see what our external environment is like and what we need to do to adapt to it, then eventually we will find that what works now no longer works and that we haven't got the ability, resources or time to change enough to keep up.

Often, because we are doing well at something, we forget to think about what else might be possible. Our thinking becomes limited to what we know, or assume we know. To illustrate this point try this task.

Join up the following nine dots in four straight lines *without* taking your pen off the paper.

Some of you will know how to do this because you have seen it before. But many of you will not realise how it's done and be unable to do it. To see how to do it, turn to the end of the chapter.

The reason that many of you can't do it immediately is because you see the shape of the nine dots as the shape of a box. You assume, even though you were not told this, that you have to stay within the shape of the box. And the problem is not solvable unless you draw your lines outside the apparent box shape.

So often we see our organisations in that box shape. 'Box' language includes things like:

'We've always done it this way.'

'It's worked for years.'

'This is what our organisation stands for.'

'This is the best way.'

'There is no other way.'

'We tried it before and it didn't work then.'

'The trustees/volunteers/staff/beneficiaries/funders won't like it.'

'Box' language creates 'box' thinking. We are unable to think of new and different ways of doing things because we are making certain assumptions about how our world will be in the future.

The Sigmoid Curve

Some of you may be familiar with the Sigmoid Curve. This curve is a mathematical expression which describes a rate of growth which is rapid and then declines. This produces a curve that appears as an S, due to this slow start. There is then a period of rapid growth, followed by a levelling out and eventually potentially declining. Many biological and ecological systems follow this structure (e.g. population growth) and its pattern has been replicated in studies of product life cycles and societal trends.

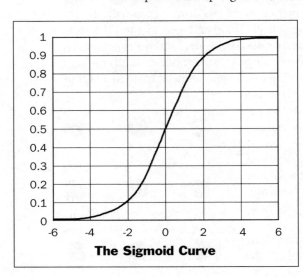

The Sigmoid Curve

The eminent writer Charles Handy believes that the Sigmoid Curve also applies to the growth and development of organisations. He argues that the best time to create the new curve for your organisation is before it peaks.[4] In some ways this is harder to do, because it is difficult to recognise the need for change (or indeed, to get others to) during a period of success. Nonetheless it is vital. Most organisations don't see the need for change until the curve is on its downward trend, which means that you begin the change process during a period of 'failure' when resources are likely to be more limited, people are likely to be demoralised and the focus will be on what's going wrong or what went wrong rather than the more important question of what's possible for the future.

So the point at which to look at creating change is when the organisation appears to be on the upper part of the trend, before it starts to level out. In fact, the most successful organisations are constantly looking to see what needs to change.

This is the point at which you will often hear people use those worn out phrases such as 'if it ain't broke don't fix it', 'don't tamper with success' and so on. The point is that it doesn't have to be broken to be useless in the future. Take video cassette recorders for example. They weren't broken, they worked perfectly well, but the pace of change means that you can't buy them anymore because the new world is DVDs and MP3 players – and that's just today. Now with the advent of, for example, Sky Plus, you don't even need a recording machine to record programmes or films from the

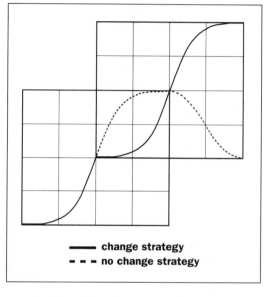

—— **change strategy**
- - - **no change strategy**

television. In fact, you don't need a separate television if you have a computer that is entertainment system enabled. We don't need floppy disks or CDs anymore to save information because we have USB memory keys. And so on.

If we don't keep up, we will be left out. It really is that simple.

Your job as a leader is to be constantly looking to the future – imagining what might be different, what the new issues might be, how what is happening in the broader context may affect what happens to your organisation and its ability to carry out its work in the longer term. You don't even need to have the answers. What you need to do is make sure that the questions are being asked.

Why are people resistant to change?

Many of us will have experienced people being resistant to change. And it is important to understand why that is. They are afraid that they might lose their jobs or their status in the organisation, or that they will end up with more work or responsibilities they don't feel ready for. And these are completely valid fears because, truthfully, change, especially big change, often involves redundancies or changes in job descriptions.

Further, change is often not handled particularly well. People are not involved in identifying the need for change, so by the time they hear about it the wheels are already in motion and people are thrust into the change process about half way through. And because they were not involved at the identification stage they tend to see proposals for change as criticism of what has gone on in the past or the quality of their current work.

So it is likely that you will meet an element of this thinking when you are proposing change. It is important that you, as the change initiator, recognise that decisions taken in the past were valid decisions based on the needs of that particular moment. If you want to de-rail your change quickly then blame the need to change on failures in the past!

People are often also afraid because they fear that change is irrevocable and that they will be stuck with something they hate and that doesn't work.

I have observed that when change is implemented there are a series of stages that people often go through in reaction to the change, which remind me of what happens during a normal grieving process.

Stage 1   Shock/surprise
Stage 2   Denial
Stage 3   Cognitive acceptance
Stage 4   Emotional acceptance
Stage 5   Engagement

Stage	Typical reactions
1 Shock/surprise	■ Perception that someone is to blame ■ Doubts in their own competence or the competence of others ■ Distrust of leaders proposing the change
2 Denial	■ Questioning the need to change ■ Arguing for the status quo ■ Pointing out the negative consequences of change ■ Grumbling and upset
3 Cognitive acceptance	■ Understanding of the rationale ■ Asking questions about process and impact ■ Arguing for alternatives
4 Emotional acceptance	■ Feeling the need ■ Few grumbles ■ Possible generation of excitement and optimism
5 Engagement	■ Involved in solutions ■ Coming up with ideas ■ Willingness to experiment ■ Willingness to learn new things

I don't think you can short cut any of these stages. But if you are sensitive to what people go through, you can minimise the damage caused at the early stages and move people faster through to engagement.

Do not underestimate the emotional impact that change has on people. And don't ignore it. If you ignore the emotional response, or dismiss it as irrelevant, you will seriously hamper your ability to see the change process through.

> GRRR... YOU COME IN HERE AND START CHANGING EVERYTHING

Nowadays organisations cannot guarantee employment; indeed, voluntary organisations and charities never have been able to. In place of this, however, we can guarantee employability. In other words we can equip our people with the ability to respond openly and willingly to change and give them the emotional skills to feel positive and excited about change, wherever they are working. So if you can help people to realise that the more they get used to change, the better equipped they are for not just the organisation's future, but also for their own, they are more likely to engage.

How to get the organisation to change

The approach that you take to initiating change is quite important. Focus on the future and what the organisation needs to look like in order to achieve the objective.

Importantly, honour the past. Help people to understand that the need for change is not necessarily due to the organisation failing to do doing things properly in the past, or due to previous poor management – or due to staff/volunteers not doing a good job. The change is in response to circumstances existing today and those that are likely to exist tomorrow.

My favourite change phrase is 'Honour the past – don't live in it'. Kriss Akabusi, the gold-medal-winning athlete says, 'The past is for reference, not residence'. I think this is a useful way of thinking and talking about why we shouldn't cling to the past. Someone once said that the difference between the voluntary sector and the private sector is that in the private sector organisations are usually looking ahead to where they're going and in the voluntary sector organisations are very often looking behind them at where they came from. That's all well and good, but while you're looking behind you and feeling proud of the past, you don't see the hole in the road that you're about to fall into.

To engage people in change, of course acknowledge history, but get them to think about how to make that 'history' last a bit longer!

To do this, involve people at the very beginning of the change process. That is *at the stage at which you think change might be necessary but you don't know what or why or how!* There are a number of techniques for doing this.

The PESTLE model

One of the ways to get people engaged in thinking about the need for change without feeling criticised is to use the PESTLE model.

Political
Environmental (I usually interpret this to mean our 'market place')
Societal
Technological
Legal
Economic

It is a way of looking at the things that affect your organisation and asking yourself what impact they will have and what you can do about it.

So you ask questions at your trustee meetings or your senior management team meetings such as:

- What is happening in the political arena at the moment? For instance, what are the local authorities' priorities for the next few years? Has there been a change in leadership of the council – what does that mean? What could we do about it?
- What is happening in our environment/market at the moment? What are the trends? Are there other charities doing the same as us? Are we the best at what we do? How could we be better?

And so on.

You should also be asking these questions of your management team, indeed of all the staff in your organisation. And certainly at the staff level you should be asking questions such as:

- What are we doing well?
- What are we doing less well?
- What are we not doing that we should be doing?
- What are we doing that we shouldn't be doing?
- What could we do differently/better for the future?

It has been my experience that if you ask staff what could be done differently they nearly always know! And if you ask them in the context of improving what you do and the way in which you do it, usually they will have lots of suggestions to make. And if you have asked them they are much more likely to participate, if not enthusiastically, then at least not reluctantly, in the change process.

However, in bringing about successful change remember to think about the following:

1 Be clear about the vision behind the change. What is this change going to achieve for the organisation?
2 What is the change motivator? That is, what is it that is happening or is going to happen that makes the change matter?
3 What is the capacity for the change? In other words, how open are people to it? What will you need to do to engage them in the process? Do you have the resources to cope?
4 First steps. What are the things that you can do to begin the change process that will feel like immediate steps and that will be 'successful'?

In terms of dealing with people's fears it is important to reassure them that if the change doesn't work then you won't stick with it. A good approach is to talk about the need to 'experiment', to 'try it out' and see if we can make it work. This approach reduces the fear that people will be stuck with something unworkable. There may be some who will see it as an opportunity to 'prove' to you that the change won't work. But the vast majority, your 'critical mass', will feel more empowered to see if they can make it work.

The Moses metaphor

I came across a great metaphor for change from two American writers, William Bridges and Susan Mitchell. This is a useful way to think about what happens during the change process.

However, do bear in mind, when thinking about change in the context of this metaphor, that change is actually continual. The common mistake that people make is thinking that if they change something, that'll be it. Actually change is continual and ongoing which is why it is so important to ensure that your people understand that you don't arrive, breathe a sigh of relief and celebrate that the change is over. It is constant.

If you know the story of Moses the key elements, in this context, are that he realised change had to happen, created the vision of a land of milk and honey and convinced the Pharaoh to let him lead his people out of Egypt. He then parted the waters of the Red Sea and they closed behind him, spent 40 years wandering around in the wilderness, found Mount Sinai and got the ten commandments, and handed over leadership to Joshua who eventually led the people to the Promised Land.

As a metaphor for change there are a number of elements to consider.

The story	What's really going on?	What can you do?
A vision of a land of milk and honey	Moses is painting a picture of a possible new future to inspire people	■ Identify the 'land of milk and honey' for your organisation – how is it going to be better and why? ■ Express it simply and clearly in a way that inspires people ■ Use language that helps your managers to emphasise continually the reason for the change in a positive way
Convincing the Pharaoh to let go	In bringing down plagues Moses was essentially highlighting the consequences of not changing	■ Consider and think about the 'inner pharaohs' ■ Anticipate people's resistance and think of ways to overcome it ■ Highlight the problems – don't rush to solve them independently of the change process – they add impetus to your change process
Parting the Red Sea	This was a big 'win' for Moses – it was a immediate first success on the journey which reinforced the action	■ Make sure you build in some early quick wins to show people that it's the right decision ■ Communicate them across the organisation
Closing the Red Sea	When the waters closed behind them there was no going back	■ Change something that can't be changed back ■ Encourage people to focus on the new direction
Wandering about in the wilderness	This was the stage at which the first push was over and they had to settle into the long journey; people got tired, dispirited and hungry, convinced they'd passed that precise bush and camel several weeks ago; not sure if the choice was the right one. They needed sustenance and hope	■ Recognise that in any change process there is a transition period when it isn't clear what's happening or how things are going or when it appears to be slow and plodding ■ Don't be tempted to rush things because people are impatient or demoralised ■ Provide 'sustenance' for your people in the form of lots and lots of information; updates on progress; consultation forums; feedback mechanisms; point out successes and acknowledge mistakes and failures ■ Keep communicating the 'land of milk and honey' message but remind people that this is a continuing process

Mount Sinai and the ten Commandments	The 'new rules' for the 'new world'	■ As soon as you can 'capture' new ways of working or processes get them written up and communicated, both in writing and orally ■ Celebrate successes
Handing over to Joshua	Recognising that a different kind of leadership is needed for the next stage	■ Let go ■ Trust others to continue the change process for you ■ Empower your managers to take more decisions and continue to think of new possibilities ■ Re-emphasise the need to keep looking for change
Arriving at the Promised Land	They get there	■ You won't! Precisely because change is ongoing. ■ Look at your environment – has your Promised Land become Egypt? ■ What's changed or is going to change in the external world that means you need to change again? ■ What new things do you need to do? ■ Keep your communications mechanisms going – feedback, consultations, improvement groups etc. ■ Keep people conscious of the constant need to change

Did it work?

Do you know what? Probably not. What I mean is that a plan is only good until you put it into action, when suddenly all sorts of things pop out of the woodwork that you hadn't anticipated. It is highly unlikely that you will have identified what needs to change, how you want it to change and by when – and then find it happens exactly as planned. This is the real world. It doesn't.

So what do you need to do? Well, have some measures of success in mind which are about the outcome, *not* the process. What do you want to be different? Is it? Don't focus necessarily on how you want it to be different. For example, if you want to improve your service to your user group, has it been improved? Who judges it? It may be that the very process of implementing your plans brought about new plans and ideas and you still effectively reached your end goal.

And above all, keep communicating with people about what's working, what isn't and what's happening next.

Managing change is like piloting a sailing ship. You almost never get to your final destination via the route you planned. The wind turns in the wrong direction and you have to tack (which means taking a sideways route) or the weather gets up and you have to stop in port a little longer than you had planned, and so on. The trick is to be responsive to what might happen, realise that you probably won't anticipate most of what might happen (who can read into the future?) and make sure your ship is light and flexible enough to respond appropriately.

Change is not simply about what actions you do or don't take. It's about what you achieve at the end.

Some critical dos and don'ts!

DO

- Involve people at the very beginning of the change process
- Initiate change by encouraging people to think about the external environment
- Keep people informed all the way through the change process
- Seek to change even if things are going well

DON'T

- Think you don't need to change
- Blame the need for change on things that were wrong in the past
- Forget to link change to the achievement of your overall vision
- Ignore people's emotional responses to change

Solution to the nine dots problem

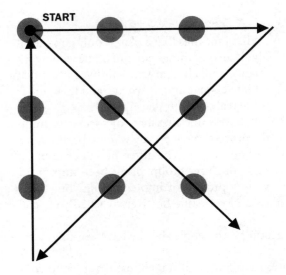

8 Networks and big set pieces

You can't stay in your corner waiting for others to come to you. You have to go to them sometimes.

A A Milne, 'Winnie the Pooh'

Outcomes

After reading this chapter you will:
- Know how to network effectively
- Have some tips and ideas about how to give really powerful presentations.

As someone at the top of the organisation it is highly likely that you are going to have to communicate in public – that is, with people outside your organisation, either formally through presentations or informally through networking. This chapter looks at how to make sure that you are credible in these environments.

Networking

If you approach each new person you meet in a spirit of adventure, you will find yourself endlessly fascinated by the new channels of thought and experience and personality that you encounter.

Eleanor Roosevelt

Networking is one of the things I, and many of the chief execs and senior people that I speak to, find the hardest thing to do – particularly when we are alone amongst strangers. But actually, it's not that hard to do if you don't think of it as a chore to be done, but rather as a way of getting to know people who you might like.

There was a senior figure in the voluntary and community sector who had the reputation of being a consummate networker because he was known to a lot of people and he made a really concerted effort to do it. However, the problem is that when he was talking to you at a function you could tell he wasn't really listening. His eyes were constantly looking over your shoulder and you felt he was looking for someone more interesting or more important to talk to. That may not have been the case, but it certainly felt like it.

People will know if you are a chore on their list or if you are only talking to them because you want something from them. And for me, networking is about creating an opportunity to build a meaningful and useful relationship – not just to have people recognise your name.

I don't think of it as networking. I think of it as making new friends, not necessarily for me personally (although that can be a rather lovely consequence of powerful networking) but for my organisation.

The classic networking mistake is to spend your time talking about your organisation. If you want people to listen to you, you have to first begin by listening to them. What's going on in their world? What are their problems? What are they interested in? You know, I've made an awful lot of professional friends by simply asking them if they were happy! I asked it, because actually I'm always curious about whether people are or not, so it's genuine. But it comes as such a surprise to people that they very often completely open up and you get the chance to forge something real rather than something expedient. However, this is just my preference. If you network for expedience only, that's probably fine. But just don't expect it to be lasting.

Also, if you are networking for relationships, then you will probably find that you don't get much in the short term. But that investment will pay off later. Oh – and don't forget – people do know if you're faking it!

The following checklist of networking is adapted from *Empower Yourself* by Eve Warren and Caroline Gielnick.

What to do	External networking
Be clear about what you want	Know what outcome you would like as a result of this networking – it may only be to have people know who you are
Approach people first	This is the really hard bit and the bit I personally hate the most. However, most of us feel uncomfortable in situations where we don't know anyone, even those who seem particularly confident. Simply start by introducing yourself and then ask about them. Who are they? Why are they at this particular event? What does their organisation do? How is it doing? Look for common ground
Give a firm handshake	This sounds a bit obvious but you'd be amazed how many people have a limp handshake or don't bother at all
Introduce positively	Speak positively about who you are and what you do. Don't assume that people will know who you are or what your organisation does. And if they don't they may feel they ought to and be too uncomfortable to ask. Tell them about the work of your organisation

Make the conversation two way	Let them do most of the talking, but make sure that you also share a little about yourself. If they have been really open and honest, reflect that back by being the same yourself
Find a way to remember them	Big problem for me! I meet a lot of people and can recognise faces but rarely names. Collect business cards. Notice something specific about them that might help you to recall them at a later date (i.e. something they once did or something you have in common)
Circulate	But not too 'obviously'. Don't spend all your time at events hanging out with the people you already know. Try to spend time with people you don't. And one of the easiest ways to do that is to invite people to join in the group that you are talking with. There is always someone on their own looking awkward. Invite them to join your group – even if you yourself are with strangers
Maintain contact after the event	This is the bit that really matters. Networking, for me, is about building up relationships. That happens after the event. A quick e-mail to say nice to meet you. A suggestion to meet for a drink or lunch

Be generous in your networking. I share my friends around. If I think there are two people who would get on well or ought to meet each other I try to make sure it happens.

Big set pieces

One of the results of your successful networking might well be that you are called upon to give a speech or formal presentation. You are likely to have to do this anyhow at some point during your leadership. The larger your organisation, the more this will be necessary, although whatever the size of your organisation, you do need to ensure that you are competent in this kind of delivery. Interestingly, big set pieces are the ones that tend to make people the most nervous and for which

they spend the most time preparing, yet actually, they are the least critical in terms of your impact on your organisation's ability to deliver. Nonetheless they are still important.

Did you know that fear of public speaking is second only to spiders in the things most feared by people? I've heard it said about public speaking that the human brain is a remarkable thing – it works from the moment you're born until the moment you stand up to speak in public!

The following advice applies whether you are delivering a set piece to your own organisation's staff or volunteers or a group of people you don't know. Making an effective public presentation begins long before you actually stand on the platform and deliver. You need to know about who your audience is and what the venue is like by answering the following questions:

Audience
- Who is your audience? What are their roles?
- If you are seeking funding or support then who is the decision maker? How do they make decisions?
- What are they interested in? And don't guess! In my early days in the voluntary sector I was asked to give a speech to about 20 chief executives of reasonably sized charities. I made an assumption that they wanted to know about the detailed make up of the voluntary sector. So that's the speech I prepared and delivered. What they actually wanted to know about was the difference in leadership behaviours between the voluntary sector and the private sector. My speech went down like a lead balloon! One phone call to the organiser would have made sure I was talking about the right thing!
- What do they already know? (In my example above, they knew more about the sector than I did!)
- What are their expectations?
- What will they have already heard? Who has spoken before you? What were they talking about? How did the audience react?
- How are they likely to listen? Are they likely to be a fairly cynical audience? Will they hang on your every word?
- In what context will they be listening? What is their state of mind? Is it the end of a long day? Have they heard loads of presentations about the same subject already?

Venue
- How is the room laid out? Where will you be in relation to your audience?
- Are you expected to stand on a platform or behind a lectern? Don't be bullied by the organisers here – if you don't like lecterns don't use them. My experience is that the most credible and interesting speakers don't read out speeches from behind a lectern. They use a lapel mike and walk about freely.
- What will the lighting levels be like? Again, here, you do not have to be spotlighted on a stage if you don't want to be. Personally, I hate it and always ask the organisers to turn on the house lights. I prefer to see who I am talking

to and gauge their reactions as I am speaking. And I would *strongly* advise against using PowerPoint for anything other than visual images, graphs or photographs – but more on that later.

Focus on the outcome

You need to be really clear about what you want to achieve as a result of your presentation as that will make a big difference to the content you include and how you deliver it.

Many people confuse the purpose of a presentation with the outcome. You should focus on what change you want to see in the audience as a result of your presentation, that is, the outcome.

Generally speaking there are six reasons for presenting:

1 To brief (update or inform)

In other words you want to impart some information. But actually the real objective is not about imparting the information, but about the audience understanding and remembering what it is you have told them. Therefore...

Outcome: to have the audience understand and retain a piece of information.

How?

- Use simple language that they will understand.
- Keep to no more than three key points – they won't remember more.
- Use real examples that they can identify with.

2 To instruct (inform or teach)

Here you want your audience to learn something – but that is specifically because you want them to do something with what they have learned. Therefore...

Outcome: to have the audience understand, remember and act on their learning.

How?

- Build in some way of them practising what they have learned.
- Build in time for them to think about or share what action they will take.

3 To inspire (inspire or motivate)

Here you want your audience to be inspired by what you have said – often, again, to bring about some kind of action. Therefore...

Outcome: to make the audience feel excited and enthused.

How?

- Use powerful, simple language.
- Tell stories.
- Avoid statistics and data.
- Use visual images.

4 To advocate (convince or sell a point of view)

Here you want your audience to be your ambassadors after your presentation, or to give you the funds or the project or the contract. Therefore...

Outcome: to get the audience to believe in your case as if it were their own – or to buy/donate/sponsor/support.

How?

- Use examples from their experience.
- Get them to imagine what it would be like if it was them in this situation/plight etc.
- Use real examples and stories.
- Show them what's in it for them.
- Appeal to the emotions.

5 To stimulate (discussion and debate)

Here you are aiming to get your audience actively engaged and drawing their own conclusions. Therefore...

Outcome: to get the audience to talk and think about the issue.

How?

- Make plenty of time during your presentation for them to talk to one another.
- Pose questions – real ones that they have to think about to answer.

6 To gratify (entertain or amuse)

Here you are aiming for the feel-good factor. Therefore...

Objective: to send them away laughing and feeling good.

How?

- If you are not a natural joke teller then don't tell jokes – tell funny stories, based on true events.
- Exaggerate to enhance the humorous aspects.
- Take the mickey out of yourself and your own experiences.

Being clear about the outcome will help you to make your presentation more powerful. For example, if you want to stimulate discussion and debate, then get your audience to speak to each other during your presentation. Build in time for them to discuss what you have said.

If you want your audience to feel inspired you might build in some kind of physical activity to get their adrenaline going, or show them a graphic photograph, or use poetry or quotations.

Always think in terms of outcomes not objectives. Objectives might indicate some of what you need to include in your content – but thinking of outcomes is more likely to produce the kinds of results you're interested in.

Structure

Structuring your presentation is in fact one of the easier aspects.

Opening

Make it punchy and memorable. Even if what you are talking about doesn't seem exciting on paper – you can make it sound exciting by how you draw attention to it in the opening part of your presentation. The following topic is not exactly inspirational, but if you compare the two openers you can see how the speaker made it seem as if it mattered.

Snooze in 5 seconds…

'During the previous fiscal year the French voluntary sector had access to in excess of 25 per cent of an EU-funded grant, voted for and agreed on by the key voice agencies in the regional development arena, with no particular bias or prejudice evident at any of the application stages. In comparing giving data for the year, it is clear that the British voluntary sector did not fare so well. Intensive investigations have led us to the conclusion that, whilst there are many factors which influence the awarding of the grant, the primary factor is the failure of the British voluntary sector to both understand and work within the clearly laid out guidelines and procedures necessary to ensure successful applications. This is a situation that we need to rectify.'

Got me awake!

'Last year the French received 25 per cent of the European Regional Development Grant. Guess what the Brits got? Three per cent! Why? Because we don't know how to use the system. This presentation is going to show you how.'

You want your audience to know immediately that what you are going to say is interesting – so don't use long words and clever jargon. Keep it punchy and try to include something that will immediately make them sit up and pay attention. And get that point in in the first few sentences.

Middle

Don't put in more than three to five key points. Any more than that and people won't remember. The fact is that most of us cram far too much information into our presentations. Why do people say too much? They may be keen to demonstrate what they know, they want to be helpful, they want to demonstrate they have done their homework or perhaps they simply love their subject and could bang on about it for hours. You need to limit the information.

If you think about it, if, during a presentation someone gave you 100 facts how many would you remember? What about ten facts? Well you might remember five per cent of 100 facts (and you have no way of ensuring that the five facts they remember are the most important ones!). Your audience might remember 50 per cent of 10 facts (but again, are they the ones you want them to remember?). So if people are only going to remember around about five facts why not only give them five facts – the ones that you actually want them to remember because you believe they are the most important.

The point is that people don't remember much of what they simply hear. So you do need to concentrate on a small number of key points. No more than five – and probably the optimum is three.

If you think about the pieces of information that had most impact on their audiences compare the following:

The Sermon on the Mount	100 words
The American Declaration of Independence	500 words
The EU Directive on aubergines	7,000 words

I rest my case!

In the main content of your presentation – *use examples*, and try to avoid making them hypothetical. Real examples, either yours or others', are much more powerful at getting your message across. Stories not stats is the rule of thumb here.

End

Make it clear that you have ended – and have a concluding sentence which is punchy and adds to the content. Always end the presentation with something like 'Thank you for listening'. That honours the audience and makes it clear that you have finished. Again, avoid long drawn-out paragraphs with loads of detail and that classic of all presenter mistakes – the neverending ending: '… and finally … oooh, and also finally … and finally, finally.'

For example: 'The British voluntary sector can achieve 50 per cent of the EU regional development grant. Thirteen billion euros! Just follow my advice. Thank you for listening.'

And finally and most importantly, as someone once said, the best way to make people think you know what you're talking about – is to know what you're talking about!

Winning your audience

If you think about the best speakers you have heard you will probably find that they share some of the following things in common. All you need to do is practise the same things. They:

- vary their pace (volume and tone differ at different points);
- speak directly to the audience;
- have plenty of eye contact;
- come across as friendly and approachable;
- seem to be natural – themselves;
- pause often;
- think before answering a question;
- smile frequently;
- use colloquialisms;
- use informal language;
- keep the number of points they make to the minimum;
- use visual imagery;
- allow the audience to use their imagination – they don't provide all the pictures for them;
- tell a story;
- avoid abstract language – you know those speakers who use big, clever language when simple words would be much easier to understand and much easier to remember.

When you are giving an oral presentation it is really important that you don't confuse language that is meant for the eye with language that is meant for the ear. Spoken language needs to concentrate on words that immediately bring visual imagery to the audience's minds. For example, what would you immediately think of if I used the term 'wealth-creation unit'? How about 'livestock asset'? Alright, what about 'bovine resource'? Well, would it be easier if I just used the term 'cow'? Get the point?

Keep your language simple and imaginable!

Visual aids

I just want to end by talking about the use of visual aids. Why do we use visual aids? Well, theoretically they are supposed to enhance our presentation. But the sad fact is that most presenters nowadays think of visual aids only as PowerPoint – which they then use as a crib sheets or a version of their speaker notes, something I truly hate.

Think about PowerPoint presentations – do they *really* enhance? Or do they actually get in the way of the personality of the speaker (almost always in my experience). Unless you have the time or energy to make your PowerPoint presentation dance and whistle I would be inclined to avoid it.

If you do want to use visual aids then use real ones. An ex-colleague of mine tells a story about starfish on a beach to illustrate the point that every small thing can make a difference. It goes like this: A mother and daughter were walking along the beach when a wave came in and deposited a load of starfish on the beach. The starfish were stranded and started dying. The little girl started picking up the starfish and throwing them back into the sea, one by one. The mother said 'What are you doing? You can't make a difference to all those starfish.' To which the little girl replied, 'No, but I'll make a big difference to this one.' At which point my colleague holds up a real starfish. Very powerful.

You could, for example, show copies of artwork, photographs, play a song and so on – much more powerful and meaningful than bullet-pointed sentences on a big screen.

So begin by assuming you don't need PowerPoint and then add it when you do. Quite apart from anything else, the eyes absorb information faster than the ears (we read at 300 words per minute and hear 120 words per minute). Therefore, if we are presented with a conflict between listening and reading – we will read. However, if you do feel the need to use PowerPoint, here are some tips:

- Cut back on the number of slides – make each one earn its place.
- Top and tail yourself – begin with *no* visuals other than yourself.
- Use blank slides in between points so the audience focuses on you.
- Keep slides simple.
- Minimise words – maximise pictures/diagrams.
- Remember alternatives to visuals – the story, examples, anecdotes, analogies etc.
- *Do not read out the slides!!!*

And, remember, the most powerful visual aid is *you!*

Questions

If handled badly, question sessions can very often scupper what was otherwise a perfectly good presentation or speech.

Here are some tips:

- Plan ahead (anticipate and rehearse).
- Don't criticise the question or the questioner.
- Acknowledge the right of the questioner to ask a question, e.g. that's a fair/interesting/new/thought-provoking/stimulating question.
- If you don't know – admit it, seek answers from others, say you will find out.
- Don't accept multiple questions if you can't handle them (and personally, as an audience member, I would always rather hear one question and one answer than try to keep track of multiple ones).
- Defer long answers to the end or afterwards.
- Don't meet hostile questions with hostility – keep calm.
- Ask for the question to be repeated.
- Take time to think (scribble the question on a piece of paper).
- Bridge from the negative to the positive (e.g. 'That's a valid point however, the real issue is… '; 'The question you should be asking is… '; 'It makes more sense to talk about…')
- Rephrase the question.
- Seek allies.
- Take questions at the end – get the audience to make notes.
- Finish on time – let others go – but you can stay behind to answer questions.
- Look around – answer everyone.
- In team presentations, agree in advance who will answer or agree the presentation 'leader' who will decide.

And finally, don't worry too much about whether people liked you or not. The real test of an effective presentation is whether or not people do something differently as a result of it.

I used to run a residential leadership programme. In those days at the end of the programme we used to judge how successful it had been by the number and quality of the action points that our delegates had identified. On one particular occasion we had a speaker talking about individual learning. Almost without exception every delegate loathed him. They thought he was patronising, out of touch and a bit of a know-it-all. However, interestingly, at the end of the programme when we shared the action points, there were more actions around individual learning than any other topic on the entire course. He had got them so cross they were actually thinking about the topic, but it was inadvertent, I must admit, as he did not intend such a negative response. I am not saying you should annoy people, simply that the true test is in what happens afterwards.

Some critical dos and don'ts!

DO

- Make friends
- Follow up with people with whom you bonded
- Concentrate on the key things you want people to remember in presentations
- Keep your presentations short and focused
- Think about your audience

DON'T

- Pretend to be interested in someone for the sake of it
- Forget to share your networks with others
- Give too much information
- Try to look clever
- Worry too much about whether they like you or not

9 Staying sane

The battles that count aren't the ones for the gold medals. The struggles within yourself – the invisible, inevitable battles inside all of us – that's where it's at.

Jesse Owens, Olympic gold medal athlete

Outcomes

After reading this chapter you will:
- **Know what causes you stress**
- **Identify some techniques for dealing with the pressure.**

We've already identified that leadership at the top is a tough job, albeit with its own rewards. For many people the challenge is emotional and mental: keeping focused on the overall aims of the organisation whilst at the same time working with human beings who can be unpredictable, while still having to be conscious that we have an enormous effect on what goes on. All this can be very stretching.

You have to be acutely self-aware to be successful as a leader. But that acute self-awareness can also make us very sensitive to those things in ourselves that we don't like much. We become very conscious of our failures and failings and it can be very easy to let that awareness distort our self-image so that we forget that actually we're pretty alright as human beings. I can tell you from my own experience that those leaders who wake up in the middle of the night agonising about where they went wrong, who beat themselves up for their mistakes, who hold themselves accountable for what goes badly are often better than those leaders who drive along, blindly indifferent to the casualties along the roadside caused by their erratic driving!

On top of your own self-analysis, you also have an enormous job to do. You are responsible for an entire organisation and will be held accountable for its success or failure, even when circumstances have been greater than your ability to influence or respond to them. And that means it can be very stressful at the top.

This chapter is primarily about what you can do as an individual to manage your own stress levels and maintain a healthy and proportionate sense of self.

What is stress?

Stress is essentially a term used to describe the pressure that is being put upon us, either internally or externally. In itself it is not necessarily a bad thing – and in fact we tend to call it 'pressure' or 'challenge' when we feel we can handle it and 'stress' when we feel we can't.

What makes the difference between whether we feel overwhelmed or challenged is largely due to our perception of what is happening to us. That is not to say that situations aren't in and of themselves intrinsically difficult. Of course they are. But how is it that some people fall apart under such circumstances, or get ill or distressed, while others appear perfectly well able to cope?

It's all about perception. Our ability to cope with stress is largely down to our perception of what is happening and our perception of our ability to deal with it.

In any aspect of our lives we have challenges which are accompanied by things we perceive as supports, and those we perceive as constraints. Constraints are those things that make us feel that the situation we are in is challenging or difficult. For example, we may be running out of funds for a particular project; we may not have the technology or resources we need; our people may be inexperienced, unskilled or unmotivated. Or we may have difficult relationships with some individuals in the organisation.

Supports are those things that we perceive as helping us. We may get a sudden influx of cash, or a new piece of equipment or a team that is working well together.

We will perceive ourselves as having stress not simply when the constraints are greater than the supports but when the challenge feels bigger than our capacity to deal with it.

The diagram below illustrates what happens to us when supports and constraints are in conflict with one another. I unashamedly stole this from a friend of mine, John Edmondson, who is one of the best psychologists in the country and an expert at stress to boot.

The diagram speaks for itself. Obviously the best place to be is in the upper right quadrant. Having said that, however, recognise that you will not always be in the 'best' place. The trick is to notice where you are and to do something about moving (perhaps even literally!).

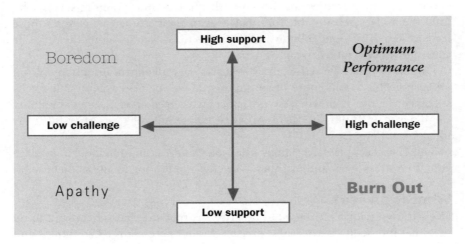

Stress is different for different people. What makes you feel challenged and excited may well cause other people real upset and difficulty. This is particularly important to recognise at the top of the organisation because it is too easy to forget that others may not be able to keep up with your vision and excitement. Further, even if you are experiencing high levels of stress, as the leader at the top you need to make sure that you are not passing on your stress to others around you.

When you are told that one of the qualities you need at the top is the ability to stay calm, that's not simply referring to your internal sense of calmness, but to your ability to disguise your stress levels from others around you. That sounds hard. And it is – but it is so important. Your role is about giving people hope and if they see you unable to cope, that will adversely affect their ability to cope themselves.

Having said all that, you are still a human being and so you need to find a way to manage and minimise your stress.

There are five main generic causes of stress:
1 Our perception of the demand placed upon us.
2 Our perception that there is no balance between the demand and the support.
3 One bit of our lives is either taking up more time and attention than we want or another bit isn't getting enough time and attention.
4 We are asked to do something which challenges our intrinsic value set.
5 We are experiencing a period of major change – whether positive or negative.

How likely are you to get stressed?
You are more likely to experience unacceptable stress if there is not at least some balance in your life, some area in which you think things are going well. I know from experience that if things are tough at work, having a healthy life outside of it really helps – and of course vice versa.

So, how do you feel about how well you are doing in all the key areas in your life (after all – you are not just a chief exec/senior manager!)? You will experience stress if there is an area which is important to you but which you do not feel is going well or on which you're not spending enough time. And at the top of the organisation it is very easy to let work dominate.

The following questionnaire is simply designed to get you to think about how happy you are overall. I have listed a few areas that typically matter to people. You may find you want to adjust the questionnaire to suit your own particular circumstance. However, the key thing here is to notice which areas are important and which are not, and how well you feel you are doing in them. If you mark something as relatively unimportant and you're not doing well at it – well so what? It's about getting some perspective and concentrating on those things that really matter.

Having said that, as your life moves and changes you will find that your priorities also change. For example, if you have fallen in love and are planning a future with someone, the chances are that will become more important than work. Or if you are at a critical point in your career, or there is some major thing happening at work, then for a period of time that might be more important than family. Don't be unrealistic. Of course ultimately, for most people, family comes first in the overall wider context, but for particular times in your life it is possible that you will need their patience and support while you concentrate on something else. I don't think there's anything wrong with that, provided that's not a permanent state of affairs and that you a) acknowledge their support and b) give it back!

How do I feel about my life?

Rank the following life areas in order of importance from 1 (being the least important) and 11 (being the most important). Then mark on a score of 1 to 5 how satisfied you are with that part of your life (with 1 being not very satisfied and 5 being very satisfied). Below is a fictitious example of what the questionnaire might look like when completed.

Life area	How important is it to me?	How satisfied am I with it?	Action?
My job	3	4	
My relationships with my immediate colleagues	9	3	
The kind of organisation I work for	4	4	
The way my career is developing	6	2	
My love life (emotional)	1	5	
My love life (physical)	11	3	
My family life	2	4	
My home (the physical environment)	7	2	
My social life	8	3	
Relationships with my friends	10	2	
My hobby or outside interest	5	1	

The important point to note is discrepancies between the two figures. Are your scoring 3s, 4s and 5s in your satisfaction of those areas you ranked in importance from 1 to 6? If you are not scoring highly in those areas that really matter to you at the moment, then that is where you need to focus your attention.

You will notice that there is an action column – the point of that is that you don't just accept those areas where you feel you are not as happy or doing as well as you would like. You do something about it!

Recognising your own symptoms of stress

So how do you know if you are over-stressed? I said earlier that stress is different for different people. It is also true that each person's symptoms of stress are different. The test is to notice changes in your own behaviour (or changes in others' behaviour if you are monitoring their stress levels). For example, perhaps you are normally garrulous and excitable and you find yourself morose and silent; or you normally pick at your food and are now scoffing it down! It is the *change* in behaviour that is critical to notice.

Test your stress levels

Read each of the statements listed below and tick those that apply to you when you are under too much stress.

- [ ] I am easily irritated
- [ ] I have difficulty concentrating for any length of time
- [ ] I feel tired even when I wake up in the morning
- [ ] I have difficulty making even simple decisions
- [ ] The quality of my sleep deteriorates. I have difficulty getting to sleep and/or I wake in the night
- [ ] I have difficulty controlling my temper
- [ ] I feel powerful negative emotions
- [ ] I feel generally run down and rather unwell
- [ ] Life seems to be hopeless. Nothing seems worthwhile and I feel really low
- [ ] My eating pattern alters. I either lose my appetite or I seem to eat more food than usual
- [ ] I have difficulty absorbing new data
- [ ] I suffer from frequent headaches
- [ ] I have difficulty recalling information when I need to
- [ ] I drink more alcohol than usual
- [ ] I experience dramatic swings of mood
- [ ] I miss or am late for appointments
- [ ] I feel wound up and unable to relax properly
- [ ] I am unable to achieve my normal level of creativity
- [ ] I suffer from backache regularly
- [ ] I feel inadequate and unable to cope
- [ ] I take time off work
- [ ] I suffer from indigestion
- [ ] I seem to lack capacity to focus on one thing at a time – my mind keeps wandering to other issues
- [ ] The least little thing sends me into a panic
- [ ] I smoke more cigarettes than usual
- [ ] I have a frequent need to urinate
- [ ] In discussion with other people I frequently repeat myself

☐ My driving is erratic and my judgement impaired

☐ I seem to spend a lot of time worrying

☐ I feel lethargic and uninterested with work and/or life

☐ I find myself more frequently arguing with my partner/family/friends

☐ I find myself uninterested in things I previously liked

If you notice that your answers to these are giving you the message that you are under too much stress then you need to do something about it. Remember, your perception is the first thing that will help. It will always be stressful at the top, what you need to work on is how you view it.

We are our own worst enemy!

My friend I mentioned earlier, John Edmondson, talks about how as human beings we can be our own worst enemies.

He talks about what he calls dysfunctional assumptions. Those are assumptions about how we should be in the world that are unrealistic and unachievable. For example, we all want to be accepted. That is a functional way to think. However, it is dysfunctional if you want to be liked all the time by everyone. That's not possible and you need to accept it.

We all want to feel in control. However, we can't be in control of everything all the time. We all want to be competent. But inevitably we will make mistakes. We feel responsible for things. But we can only be responsible for what we do, not for what others do. We want to be in control of our emotions, but sometimes we will get angry and emotional and want to cry or shout.

The point is that we need to accept the fact that we are human beings and that we are not perfect. It sounds so obvious – but is often so difficult for us to accept. We engage in thought processes that can make things worse for us.

Are you guilty of any of the following?

Awfulising

This is when we imagine the worst about a situation. You know, something goes wrong at work or a mistake is made. You immediately assume you'll get the sack. And you'll feel so bad about yourself that you won't be able to find another job. You'll end up defaulting on your mortgage and being made homeless. Your partner will leave you for someone else and you'll end up on the streets – drinking too much... Recognise any of this? And this all happens in about 0.2 of a second!

Action:

- Give yourself a reality check.
- Focus on the moment you are in – not the moment that may or may not come!

Musterbating (should/must/ought)

This one of my favourite John Edmondson expressions: the rigid thinking. You know – things must be done right, people must do as they're told, meet deadlines, do a good job, not make mistakes and so on. The reality of the world is that people don't always do what they should, meet their deadlines or clean up their mistakes.

Action:
- Allow for mistakes to happen.
- Look at what can be done to put it right or avoid it next time.
- Forgive, forgive, forgive!

Mind reading

This is where we imagine we know what people are thinking. We walk into a room of trustees and one of them appears to frown at us. We immediately assume that they've found out something and we're going to get into trouble!

Action:
- Ask people outright what they are thinking.
- Question them in response to their body language if it appears to you to be negative.

Over-generalising

Over-generalising is about making something worse than it really is. We made a mistake and think that everyone is going to think that we're rubbish at everything. Or one small thing goes wrong and we extrapolate it into complete disaster.

Action:
- Give yourself a reality check.
- Get a sense of perspective – how will you feel in a week, a month, ten years, on your death bed – will it really matter then?

Underestimating our skills

This is an absolute classic. Marcus Aurelius once said something along the lines of, 'we will use the same skills and abilities to solve the problems of tomorrow as we used to deal with the difficulties of today'. We didn't get to where we are today without having the ability to problem-solve and whatever we are faced with, we will still be able to deal with it. Honest!

Action:
- Remind yourself of how you have dealt successfully with similar situations before.
- Trust your abilities.

Focusing on how we feel not what we do

As human beings we are driven by our emotions. We are conscious of our reactions to things, we know how we feel inside. And this can very often make us forget about the fact that no one knows how we are feeling unless we show them. For example, chances are that if you are nervous giving a public presentation, no one even notices and you do a good job anyway. How you feel is not the issue here, it's what you do. You can do a great job and be terrified. The great job is the bit that matters!

Action:
- Concentrate on what you are doing not how you are feeling.

Forgetting to solve the problem

Another classic. We get so wrapped up in how awful it is we forget that we can do something about it. Our latest communication with staff has been horribly misinterpreted. Well, go and communicate again and get it right this time. Our trustees have gone nuts over something we did without checking with them first – well go and clean it up.

Action:
- Solve the blooming problem – change the situation.
- And if you can't solve it – accept it.

Reinforcing our misery

This is when we focus on all the things that are bad, or we do things that contribute to that bad feeling. A lovely example is my friend Deborah. She was having a dinner party and rang me up, late in the afternoon, horribly stressed and in tears saying she couldn't cope and could I please come over and help out. I arrived to discover that she had really loud 'techno' music blasting out throughout the house. Nothing wrong with that – but I doubt it was contributing to a sense of calmness and well-being!

Action:
- Make sure that you are not adding to the problem by doing things that make it worse.
- Ask for help.

Tips for keeping a sense of perspective

I think that, of all of the many pieces of useful advice that can be given about staying sane and relatively stress-free, the most useful is about keeping a sense of perspective. The following tips should help you to achieve that.

If you are in a difficult situation that is causing you worry then change the way you see it:

- Write down the thing that is causing you stress.
- Write down how it is making you feel.
- Write down how your feelings are influencing your behaviour and your ability to gain some 'perspective'.
- Ask yourself the question – 'What is the worst thing that could happen?'
- Then ask yourself – 'If the worse happens, what can you do?'
- Ask yourself – 'How likely is it that the worst thing will happen?'
- Then ask yourself 'What is most likely to happen?'

If you do this you will probably find that the situation is not nearly as bad as it seems at the time. Remember: worry does not rob today of its sorrow, it robs tomorrow of its strength.

Build up and use a strong personal support network

Make sure you have support mechanisms in place to help you to deal with difficult times. You must not try to be over-dependent or too self-reliant. Talking to someone about what is bothering you can often help you to see the wood for the trees and put things into perspective. Bottling up emotion rarely helps and can often make things worse.

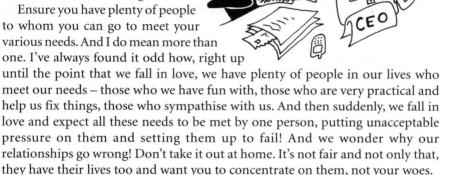

Ensure you have plenty of people to whom you can go to meet your various needs. And I do mean more than one. I've always found it odd how, right up until the point that we fall in love, we have plenty of people in our lives who meet our needs – those who we have fun with, those who are very practical and help us fix things, those who sympathise with us. And then suddenly, we fall in love and expect all these needs to be met by one person, putting unacceptable pressure on them and setting them up to fail! And we wonder why our relationships go wrong! Don't take it out at home. It's not fair and not only that, they have their lives too and want you to concentrate on them, not your woes.

Fill in the following – and if you find it's only one or two names – have another think. If you are always using the same people you will usually get the same answers!

	Name
Who can I rely on in a crisis?	
Who makes me feel good about myself?	
Who can I be totally myself with?	
Who can give me honest feedback in a way that I can accept?	
Who can I talk to when I am worried about work?	
Who can I talk to when I am worried about home?	
Who is able to make me stop and think about what I am doing?	
Who helps me put things into perspective?	
Who is good fun to be with?	
Who helps me take my mind off things?	
Who introduces me to new people/ideas/opportunities?	

Use your support network regularly – not just in times of crisis.

Deal with the problem

For any stressor there is normally a cause or an event which may or may not be within your control. The first thing to do is to see if you can remove the cause of the stress. For example, if you get stressed about the fact that trains are frequently late you're probably heading for trouble!

If you can't remove the cause then you need to find a way to detach yourself from it. So on your list if there are things over which you have no control – then don't worry about them – accept it and move on.

The meditative stuff

Quiet reflection and meditation doesn't work for everyone. However, there are some quick, simple things you can do to get yourself back into control in those immediate short-term moments of stress that can be difficult to deal with. Here are a couple of techniques to help you to gather yourself together quickly before you react.

Focusing outside the moment

Go to a window or a door or look at a picture or a plant. Really look at it, focus on it, the colour, the shape, the texture – continue to look at it until you feel your heart rate slowing down, your breathing becoming more measured.

Going to the quiet place

Close your eyes and imagine that you are walking through a door. Outside the door is a large field full of tall waving grass. You are walking through the grass, the sun is shining and there is a gentle breeze. The grass begins to gradually thin and you come to a small gently trickling stream. There is a pleasantly shady spot under a willow on the bank with a soft mossy base. You sit down on the moss which is soft and comfortable. You close your eyes and feel the gentle breeze on your face and in your hair, a soft warmth from the sun on your skin and you hear the whisper of the leaves on the trees and the soft trickling of the stream. You feel peaceful, calm and safe.

This is just a trick for you – you can imagine your own place.

Five-stage plan for dealing with stress

This is a simple way of pulling together what we have talked about so far.

1. Understanding and acceptance of self

- Accept that you are human and will make mistakes.
- Learn your own values and priorities.
- Accept your limitations.
- Recognise your stressors.
- Focus on your strengths.

We will meet the problems of tomorrow with the same tools that we used to solve the problems of yesterday.

Marcus Aurelius

2. Tackle the problem

- Identify the stressor.
- Attempt to change it.
- If you're unable to change it – accept it.
- If you're unable to accept it – move on.

Please give me the serenity to accept the things I cannot change, the courage to change the things I can, and the wisdom to know the difference.

Reinhold Niebuhr

3. Self-nurturing

- Treat yourself to things you like doing.
- Look after your physical well-being.
- Spend time with people who make you feel good.

No one can make you feel inferior without your consent.

Eleanor Roosevelt

4. Emotional expression

- Develop a support network.
- Engage in two-way conversations with your manager.
- Accept that the appropriate expression of emotion is fine.
- Maintain a sense of humour.

Without the human community one single human being cannot survive.

The Dalai Lama

5. Active distraction or quiet reflection

- Do something at the end of each day to mark the distinction between home and work.
- Do something that requires mental effort so that you can't think about what is stressing you (e.g. play chess, read a book or play a sport).
- Take some time to give yourself mental space.

Silence is the element in which great things fashion themselves together, that at length they may emerge, full formed and majestic, into the daylight of life.

Kahlil Gibran, Lebanese poet

Finally remember these two things:

It's not the falling down it's the staying down...

and...

Worse things happen at sea!

Some critical dos and don'ts!

DO	DON'T
■ Keep a sense of perspective ■ Build up a support network ■ Remember that you are a human being ■ Focus on what you can do rather than how you feel ■ Maintain a sense of humour	■ Let one aspect of your life dominate for too long ■ Forget to use it ■ Beat yourself up for making mistakes ■ Forget to solve the problem ■ Lose sight of what really matters

10 The gift to see us as others see us

I asked a number of chief executives I know who, I have observed generally, appear to do the right things in their organisations (that is not to say they're perfect – no one is) what would be their key messages to share with other chief executives, or what they wish they'd known when they set out on their leadership journey. This chapter prints, pretty much verbatim, what they said. I hope you find their insights and comments as useful and inspiring as I did. At the very least, you will notice that there are some similar themes running throughout each piece of advice.

In no particular order:

Fiona Ellis, Chief Executive, Northern Rock Foundation
- When under pressure fight the temptation to go into your bunker and solve all the problems yourself – your team will want to help and usually can.
- You may think you are, and want to be, unthreatening and approachable but never underestimate junior staff members' desire to please you and say what they think you want to hear – dig a little deeper to make sure you've got the real story.
- Work with everyone who is willing to work with you – you'll achieve more.
- Remember to celebrate success with your team, from the junior who gets an NVQ up to the programme that delivers fabulous results – but not to appear arrogant!
- Walk around the office and chat to everyone at least once a week but not at the same time every week.

Pat Ryan, Chief Executive, Hestia Housing Association
- Sense of humour.
- Trusting your own judgement.
- Sorting out the finances…and reminding people how important it is.
- Being willing to stand alone…trying to bring people with you of course!!!!
- Praise people and remember the little things…

Susan Daniels, National Deaf Children's Society (NDCS)
- Be clear about your goals and single minded in their pursuit.
- Appoint the very best people and take advantage of opportunities that arise.
- When mbarking on any new venture, talk to those who have already done something similar; listen and learn.
- Support others climbing up the ladder.
- Trust your instincts – if in doubt, don't.

Fiona Dawe, Chief Executive, YouthNet UK

- It's all about them – at the top you are in the field of managing human relationships. Beneficiaries or clients, staff, volunteers, the board, funders, partners, customers – team work is vital, so listen hard and appreciate well.
- Be courageous – deal with, confront, sort out the difficult people and situations. It's your job and if you don't no one else will.
- Create conditions so that everyone feels safe – then everyone behaves better, takes responsibility, takes risks. People are more creative, more likely to achieve their goals and ambitions and have more fun. Your organisation will be more productive.
- Make sure you get the money right – you can't do anything without it. And especially in small to medium-sized companies, we turn on a sixpence. You can't plan or think strategically if you don't know what's round the corner.
- Love what you do – be passionate about the mission; love the people and let them love you back. Don't do it 'for the money' if you ever can help it. It's a hard enough job and it will distort your mission. And always have a life outside work.

John Low, Chief Executive, RNIB

- Know where you are going – inspire others by describing the promised land.
- Assess whether your existing team is capable of getting you there – if not, change them, immediately.
- Don't be afraid of uncertainty, ambiguity and risk but always seek to minimise it.
- Celebrate success to the rafters but tackle poor performance quickly.
- Measure and communicate your impact to the world.

Fiona Reynolds, Chief Executive, National Trust

- Have a clear vision and stick to it.
- Communicate, comunicate, communicate.
- Build a strong team.
- Recruit people with strengths to match your weaknesses.
- Don't sacrifice work–life balance.

Kathleen Duncan, Chief Executive, Lloyds TSB Foundation

- Listen.
- Consider that you may be wrong.
- Let staff have freedom to 'fly' and support them – don't micro manage.
- Be positive.
- Say 'thank you'.

Andrew Hind, Chief Executive, Charity Commission

- Complete clarity about the organisation's vision and mission is a prerequisite for success.
- Then be clear about what success will look like and how you're going to measure it.

- Encourage leadership at all levels in the organisation, not just from what is conventionally thought of as the 'top'.
- Talk up your organisation's achievements externally but make sure rhetoric isn't ahead of reality.
- Be passionate about your organisation's cause but make strategic decisions dispassionately.

Deborah Annetts, Chief Executive, Dignity in Dying (formerly VES)

- Do not rush into making a decision – give yourself enough headspace to make the right decisions.
- Sometimes doing nothing is the right decision.
- Be clear on your vision and make sure everyone in the organisation understands and supports the vision.
- Obtain clarity as to the role of the board and the executive team.
- Mix with other CEOs – this will give you back your much-needed perspective even in the toughest of times.

Jeanette Allen, Chief Executive, MedicAlert

- When you first start a CEO role, write down your first impressions and keep them, it can be very motivating later on, especially on the inevitable darker days, to look back and see what you've achieved. Also spend most of your time at the beginning reading if possible, especially if you have come in from the outside, give yourself the opportunity to become as expert as possible in your organisation as quickly as possible. This not only helps you but it helps your senior team to trust and respect your decisions. Having said that, you are unlikely to be an expert in all the fields you manage so ensure that you delegate appropriately and use expert external sources to sanity-check key areas.
- Try to keep fresh eyes for as long as possible; once you've been there a long time, use newer staff and trustees to help keep your view of the organisation, its strengths, weaknesses and its potential fresh.
- Ensure you have or, if necessary, recruit the best possible PA and be prepared to pay them properly. It is invaluable to have a trusted, organised, intelligent assistant who acts as your gate keeper and confidante. Remember that your mood, facial expressions and tone of voice have a disproportionate impact on the staff team and you need someone to tell you when it would be best if you worked from home on any particular day!
- Get a peer group. Join networks that introduce you to other CEOs. You are not alone…
- Take the time to get to know your chair properly, how they work, how they communicate and what their expectations are of you. My first chair wrote e-mails in capitals, it took some time to understand that he wasn't shouting at me, he simply didn't know how to switch Caps Lock off!

Frank Steer, Director General and Chief Executive, Institute of Quality Assurance

- Do not blame.
- Do not bully.
- Do show respect for those with whom you work and gain their respect in return.
- Lead by example.
- Set standards and see they are maintained.

Kevin Curley, Chief Executive, NACVS

- Recruit a small team of senior managers who share your vision.
- Invest in your chair and trustees so that they understand the vision and are there for you when you need them.
- In your first few weeks get out a lot – meet your members/users and your funders.
- Build the confidence of your members/users by sending them a lot of brief information frequently and asking for their views on what they expect from their national organisation.
- Put income generation processes in place early on because they will take at least 12 months to bring a return.

Neil Betteridge, Chief Executive, Arthritis Care

- At times of change, consult on the 'how' not the 'if': prolonged uncertainty leads to destructive insecurity.
- Insist your colleagues use e-mail titles to indicate the status of the communication ('for response', 'for info' etc.), especially around periods of leave when you will return to the inevitable glut.
- Carry at all times a small notepad to capture those ideas and morsels of information you pick up at receptions and other events.
- E-mail first thing and last thing: don't get drawn into seductive sessions of ping pong. In between, use at least some part of every day for strategic thought where you can deploy a critical distance above the hoi-polloi.
- Above all, be good at who you are. If you are clearly comfortable in your skin people may still disagree with you but those worth having on board will never disrespect you.

Quentin Elston, Chief Executive, Bath Municipal Charities and St Johns Hospital

- Be generous and conduct your business with justice, mercy and compassion.
- The basis upon which you judge others will form the basis upon which you are judged.
- Similarly, with the measure you use, will be measured to you.
- First impressions do count.
- We have two ears and one mouth – listen before you speak.
- Never fool yourself that you have got the measure of something or in particular, someone.

- Acknowledge that you can't know everything and be prepared to learn.
- Undertake your own skills assessment and build a team around you to fill in the gaps.
- Trust your team.
- Value your team.
- Be prepared to allow your team to develop and take credit for their successes.
- Treat others with respect.
- Avoid toxic relationships.
- Retain a sense of balance.
- Always accentuate the positive, whilst being realistic.
- Always seek to improve.
- Take time out to refresh yourself.
- Seek perfection, but be prepared to acknowledge that it is not always possible.

Epilogue: so are you any good?

How do you judge whether or not you're doing a good job? How do you know whether or not you're an effective chief exec or senior person?

Is it the size of the balance sheet? Is it that you've grown the organisation or kept it small and focused? Is it that your trustees think you're good? Or that your staff do? Or your beneficiaries/service users? Is it that you've attracted funding, or built up huge reserves? Or that you've spent the reserves wisely and well on delivering the organisation's objectives? Are you managing the assets well – or selling them off because they're a distraction from the real work of the charity? Are you well known? Are you influencing national policy – or keeping focused locally?

Some will say the only test of your leadership is if you delivered the organisation's objectives. But does that make you good if, in doing that, you sacrificed your people, treated them unfairly or that in your ruthless determination to achieve the results you overlooked the human context? It's not that simple, is it?

Here's the thing. Different people will have different perceptions about how successful you are as a chief exec. So who's right? Well all of them and none of them. Whether you're lauded or lambasted, feted or fired, at the end of the day the only one who can really judge is you.

The *only* real test is if you can look deep into your heart, face yourself in the mirror and be able to say: 'I hung on to my integrity. I didn't hold anything back. I gave it my all. I did the best that I was able. I was courageous and humble'.

And in the end, can you say, 'My soul is intact'?

Chief execs' checklist of key questions

- Do you have an performance management system?
- Do you have a clear vision? Has this been communicated?
- Do you have a strategy for delivering your vision? Is it written down? Is there a clearly understood plan to achieve it?
- Do you meet at least monthly with your senior team?
- Do you have a clearly defined set of values with associated 'behavioural measurements'?
- Do you meet with your chair at least monthly?
- Do you delegate authority down the organisation?
- Do you have a strategy for raising funds?
- Does your senior team prepare and monitor its own budgets and performance?
- Do you have an effective mechanism for communicating with staff? volunteers? beneficiaries? trustees?
- Do you regularly update your funders on your progress?
- Do you have ways of measuring how effective your organisation's work is?
- Do you regularly network with other chief execs and key players in your field of work?
- Do you regularly review the structure of the organisation to ensure that it is right for the present and the future?
- Do you ensure that you have access to the professional expertise you need (e.g. charity law, employment law, finance, etc.)?
- Have you trained your managers in management and leadership skills?
- Do you plan in time to think?
- Are you keeping up with changes in the wider context in which you operate?
- Are you happy?

A voluntary sector aptitude test for chief executives

The Chief Executive of MedicAlert, Jeanette Allen, shared a variation of this with me and I thought it was so amusing I've included an abridged version, hoping that it will make you smile too!

Do you have what it takes to be a chief exec?

1. Can you fake a smile convincingly all day long?
2. Can you read a paragraph and make it sound as if you've read the whole thing?
3. Can you use your fingers to add up and take away, without anyone noticing?
4. Can you draw a line, stick to it, then move it and pretend it was there all along?
5. Can you look as if you're listening even when you're miles away?
6. Can you manage an agenda so that the stuff that will make your trustees mad doesn't have enough time allocated to it?
7. Can you use Google?
8. Can you convince someone that you recognise them even though you haven't got a clue who they are and suspect you don't remember them because you didn't want to?
9. Can you fool people into believing you know what you're talking about?
10. Can you call a plumber?

Bibliography, recommended reading and references

Bibliography and recommended reading

Allcock Tyler, Debra, *High Flying*, 2002, Spiro Press

Anderson, James and Ricci, Marilyn (eds), *Society & Social Science*, 1995, Open University Press

Chait, Richard P; Ryan, William P and Taylor, Barbara E, *Governance as Leadership*, 2005, John Wiley & Sons

Cook, Liz and Rothwell, Brian, *The X&Y of Leadership*, 2000, The Industrial Society

Davis, Stan and Meyer, Christopher, *Blur – the speed of change in the connected economy*, 1998, Capstone Publishing

Eastwood, Mike, *The Charity Trustees Handbook*, 2003, Directory of Social Change

Forrest, Andrew and Tolfree, Patrick, *Leaders – the Learning Curve of Achievement*, 1992, The Industrial Society

Goleman, Daniel, *Emotional Intelligence*, 1996, Bloomsbury Publishing

Hackman, Richard, *Leading Teams: Setting the Stage for Great Performances*, 2002, Harvard Business School Press

Harris, John *The Good Management Guide for the Voluntary Sector*, 2002, NCVO

Hawkins, Peter, *The Wise Fool's Guide to Leadership*, 2005, O books

Hind, Andrew, *The Governance and Management of Charities*, 1995, Voluntary Sector Press

Hudson, Mike, *Managing at the Leading Edge*, 2003, Directory of Social Change

Hudson, Mike, *Managing Without Profit*, 2002, Directory of Social Change

Johnson, Dr Spencer, *Who Moved My Cheese?*, 2002, Vermillion

Lawrie, Alan, *Developing Your Organisation*, 2000, Directory of Social Change

Lawson, Ian, *Leaders for Tomorrow's Society*, 1999, The Industrial Society

Lewin, Roger, *Regime, Birute, The Soul at Work*, 1999, Orion Press

Management Skills, 1993, Industrial Society

McMaster, Michael D, *The Intelligence Advantage, Organising for Complexity*, 1995, Knowledge Based Development Co

Morris, Desmond, *The Human Zoo*, 1994, Vintage

Olivier, Richard and Janni, Nicholas, *Peak Performance Presentations*, 2004, Spiro Press

Olivier, Richard, *Inspirational Leadership, Henry V and the Muse of Fire*, 2002, Spiro Press

Pinker, Stephen, *How the Mind Works*, 1997, Penguin Books

Ranken, Wendy Blake, *The Good Employment Guide*, 2005, Directory of Social Change

Robinson, David, *Unconditional Leadership*, 2004, Community Links

Rowntree, Derek, *The Manager's Book of Checklists*, 1996, Pearson Education Ltd

Smith, Edwin Percy, *Manager as a Leader*, 1977, Industrial Society

Taylor, Gill, *Managing Conflict*, 1999, Directory of Social Change

Turner, David, *Liberating Leadership*, 1998, The Industrial Society

White, Sir Peter, *Preparing for the Top*, 1990, The Industrial Society

References

1. Marr, Andrew, *My Trade*, 2004, Pan Books, pp. 183–184

2. Lukes, S., *Power: a radical view*, 1974, Macmillan, pp. 10–25

3. McGough, Roger, 'The Leader', *Sky in the Pie*, 1985, Puffin Books

4. Handy, Charles, 'Elephants and Fleas: Is Your Organization Prepared for Change?, *Leader to Leader* 24, Spring 2002: pp. 29–33

Organisations

Association of Chief Executives of Voluntary Organisations (ACEVO)
www.acevo.org.uk

Business in the Community (BITC)
www.bitc.org.uk

Charities Aid Foundation (CAF)
www.cafonline.org

Charity Commission
www.charity-commission.gov.uk

Directory of Social Change (DSC)
www.dsc.org.uk

Institute of Fundraising (IOF)
www.institute-of-fundraising.org.uk

Media Trust
www.mediatrust.org

National Association of Councils for Voluntary Service (NACVS)
www.nacvs.org.uk

National Council of Voluntary Organisations (NCVO)
www.ncvo-vol.org.uk

ProHelp
www.prohelp.org.uk

The Work Foundation
www.theworkfoundation.com

Volunteering England
www.volunteeringengland.org.uk

Index